Your Towns and Cities in

Nottingham
in the Great War

Dedication

This book is dedicated to all those who endured the Great War, not just the soldiers who gave their lives or those that survived but were damaged, but also to the men, women and children at home who carried on carrying on until the end was reached, ensuring that survivors had a home and work to return to. Without all of those people my life would not be lived with the freedoms I enjoy today.

Your Towns and Cities in the Great War

Nottingham in the Great War

Carol Lovejoy Edwards

Pen & Sword
MILITARY

First published in Great Britain in 2015 by
PEN & SWORD MILITARY
an imprint of
Pen and Sword Books Ltd
47 Church Street
Barnsley
South Yorkshire S70 2AS

ISBN 978 1 78383 190 6

A CIP record for this book is available from the British Library

Printed and bound in England
by CPI Group (UK) Ltd, Croydon, CR0 4YY

Typeset in Times New Roman by Chic Graphics

Pen & Sword Books Ltd incorporates the imprints of
Pen & Sword Archaeology, Atlas, Aviation, Battleground, Discovery, Family History, History, Maritime, Military, Naval, Politics, Railways, Select, Social History, Transport, True Crime, Claymore Press, Frontline Books, Leo Cooper, Praetorian Press, Remember When, Seaforth Publishing and Wharncliffe.

For a complete list of Pen and Sword titles please contact
Pen and Sword Books Limited
47 Church Street, Barnsley, South Yorkshire, S70 2AS, England
E-mail: enquiries@pen-and-sword.co.uk
Website: www.pen-and-sword.co.uk

Contents

Acknowledgements

I am raising a glass to all of those people who lived during the Great War and whose stories, in part, appear within these pages. Without them I would have nothing to write about!

I am heartily grateful for all the help and suggestions for further research given to me by the staff at Nottinghamshire Archives and Nottinghamshire Local Studies library. I would also like to thank my friends and family for pretending to listen each time I tell them about something fascinating I have found during my research.

Special thanks go to my very own wrinklies, Marion and David Henson, for their food parcels and petrol supplies during this endeavour. Where would I be without you?

Last but not least thanks go to Dr Elisabeth Blagrove and Mum, Wendy, for keeping me sane these last few years. 'Hello Birmingham, this is Nottingham calling!'

Picture the Past

In the past, anyone wanting to view the collections of hundreds of thousands of old images in the libraries and museums of Derbyshire or Nottinghamshire would have had to travel many miles to try and track down the ones they were interested in. This proved to be frustrating and time-consuming for researchers, a barrier to anyone from further afield and damaging to the more fragile images due to all the handling. The collections include photographs, slides, negatives, glass plates, postcards and engravings recalling the history of our local communities over the past hundred years and more.

Thankfully, staff in four local authorities got their heads together to solve the problem, and the idea of conserving the images using digitisation, while at the same time giving people all over the world access to the digitised versions, was conceived. With initial funding from the Heritage Lottery at the beginning of 2002, the four partner authorities, Derbyshire and Nottinghamshire County Councils and the City Councils of Derby and Nottingham set up the project.

Local studies staff in the libraries and museums started collating images and information ready for inclusion in the project and sent out thousands of letters requesting copyright clearance from the original photographers or their relatives. Nick Tomlinson was appointed as project manager to lead a team of experienced professionals inputting the information into a custom-built database and carefully digitising the images.

The Picture the Past website (www.picturethepast.org.uk) was launched in June 2003 and by the beginning of 2013 over 100,000 pictures had been added. It now attracts well over 15,000 visitors each month from all over the world.

The site is updated on a regular basis and actually gives the user the ability to 'correct' existing information or add more information to those pictures with scant details.

Designed to be as easy to use as possible, the website includes a simple keyword search facility as well as more comprehensive search mechanisms for users looking for images with a particular theme or by a specific photographer. Visitors can print out low resolution copies for their own personal use or study purposes, but for those users wanting to own a top-quality photographic copy the website includes an online ordering service with all the income raised from this service going back into the conservation and preservation of more original pictures.

This book includes just a handful of the images that appear on the website and it is very much hoped that you will go on to enjoy some of the other pictures online.

The website can be viewed at **www.picturethepast.org.uk**

CHAPTER 1

1914: Eager for a Fight

Background

In June 1914 the King and Queen visited Nottingham. Lottie Martin, aged 15 at the time, remembered, 'It was in the month of June that Queen Mary and George V made a visit to Nottingham. I remember well standing at the main gates of Wollaton Hall on Derby Road, the bottom of Hill Side, to see them enter the grounds of the residence of Lord Middleton. How lovely she looked in an open landau dressed in a lovely blue dress holding a small parasol over her head. It was a glorious day and both Flo and myself had summer dresses on. I remember mine was pink sprinkled with little blue rosebuds, the skirt was draped. How I loved it. It really made me look good, the pale pink seemed to bring a little colour to my pale cheeks. I remember that material was four pence and three farthings a yard from Meakins and Lottie Harris who had a small shop on City Road made it for me. That dress I shall never forget.'[8]

At the beginning of August 1914 the world was on the brink of war although our local paper, the *Nottingham Evening Post*, was still optimistic that it would be avoided. News of the imminent war was not shouted from the front page like today's headlines. Not until page five was the crisis revealed. The headline said 'King intervenes in Crisis' and the *Post* stated that the King had despatched a 'telegraphic

King George V and Queen Alexandra June. Courtesy of Roni Wilkinson.

communication to the Czar in reference to the international situation. Consequently a more hopeful feeling prevails.' The actual content of the telegram was not revealed. Unfortunately in the complicated political situation that was 1914 Europe, the King's words, whatever they were, were not enough to halt the storm.

France was more convinced of war and Paris newspapers reported that war was imminent and feared that it would be the worst war the world had ever seen. That turned out to be an eerily accurate prediction. The *Echo de Paris* stated that Germany had no motive for its intended attack on France, Britain knew that and would side with France. Both countries were making last ditch efforts to maintain a peaceful Europe although it seemed that the whole world was lining up on one side or the other.

Two days after these headlines in the *Echo* the *Post* reported that the British Fleet was cleared for action and Belgium had been drawn in to the war. And so began the European nightmare that turned into the First World War.

Up until the death of Archduke Franz Ferdinand on 28 June 1914 the main stories making headlines in the press were of the Irish 'situation' and of the Suffragette movement. Millicent Fawcett founded the National Union of Women's Suffrage in 1897. She believed in peaceful protest and that any violence would persuade men that women could not be trusted with the vote. She argued that if women could sit on school boards they could be trusted to vote and if they had to adhere to the laws of the land they should have a say in making those laws. If women had to pay taxes as men did they should have the same rights. Her progress was slow as most men in Parliament believed women would just not understand how it worked. This made women angry and in 1903 Emmeline Pankhurst, wanting speedier progress, founded the Women's Social and Political Union with her daughters Christabel and Sylvia.

Although the Suffragettes, as they became known, started off peacefully, they were prepared to use violence. This change came when Christabel Pankhurst and Annie Kenney interrupted a meeting to question two politicians and shouted at them when they refused to answer. The women were arrested for causing an obstruction and a technical assault on a police officer. Both women went to prison rather than pay a fine.

The Suffragettes burned down churches, vandalised Oxford Street and attacked politicians. However, in August 1914 Emmeline Pankhurst instructed the women to stop their campaign of violence and support the government in any way they could. This probably did more to persuade the government to give them the vote than any of their previous actions.

The war gave women the opportunity to take on traditionally male jobs such as tram drivers, window cleaners and munitions workers. They showed that they were just as good as the men and helped women to get the vote at the end of the war. It was a limited right to those over thirty, but a starting point nonetheless.

As regards Ireland, Colonel Seeley, former Secretary of State for War, accused the Irish Bishop of Down of accumulating guns and stirring up trouble in Ireland. The Bishop of Down vehemently denied this, claiming that he had been doing everything in his power to calm the situation. The Home Rule Act (officially called the Government of Ireland Act) was passed in September 1914. It was designed to establish a devolved government but was postponed by a Suspensory Act simultaneously and then repealed in 1920 without ever being implemented, replaced by the Government of Ireland Act 1920. This was a huge blow to the Irish who had campaigned hard for Home Rule. In 1910 the Irish Nationalists held the balance of power in their hands after general elections in January and December left the Liberals and Conservatives equally matched. The Irish Parliamentary Party agreed to back the Liberals in return for the Home Rule bill by which bicameral parliament was to be set up and a reduced number of Irish MPs would continue to sit in the Westminster Parliament.

Not all Irish MPs were disappointed. Those in Ulster were largely opposed to Home Rule. On 13 January 1913 the Ulster Volunteer Force was set up and on 25 November of that year the Nationalists set up the Irish Volunteers. In March 1914 many Army officers refused to fight the Ulster Volunteers and resigned instead. Eventually a compromise was reached and in July 1914 a number of Ulster counties were excluded from the Home Rule Act. The Suspensory Act 1914 postponed the previous Act for the duration of the war. The problem was not resolved, merely shelved and left to stew, resulting in the Easter Rising of 1916 and the resumption of hostilities after the war ended.

In 1914 the *Nottingham Evening Post* was half a penny for four pages. The front page of the newspaper was given over to advertisements. Those looking for work, holiday apartments, motor vehicles, dressmakers, milliners, furniture and baby carriages all had to look only at the first page rather than towards the back of the paper as we are used to doing now. This changed on 5 August, the day after war began. The *Post* lead with a picture of Robin Hood (7th Battalion, Sherwood Foresters) officers assembling at the Drill Hall. The headlines were all war related – 'German Warship Captured'; 'Operations in Belgium'; 'French Success'; and 'German Retreat'; words that would become too familiar in the following four years.

What made this war even more troubling was the fact that Kaiser Wilhelm II of Germany was Queen Victoria's grandson, and his mother, also Victoria, was English. What began as a family feud, for Wilhelm, escalated into uncontrollable hatred which would lose Wilhelm his Empire. He had developed a hatred for his mother which extended to England, the country of her birth, and the English. This

Home Rule Demonstration. Courtesy of Nottingham Historical Film Unit and www.picturethepast.org.uk. NTGM014755

hatred seems to stem from Vicky's, as Victoria was known, attempts to cure his disability. He had been born with a withered left arm due to a difficult breech birth. Erbs palsy is a form of nerve damage now rare. From six months on Vicky had tried everything from the weird to the wonderful to cure his arm. His arm was inserted into the still warm body of a dead hare in the hope the warm blood would feed some vitality into his arm; he had his good arm tied behind his back when he walked to make him use the damaged left arm; he was subjected to daily electrotherapy treatments and for two years he was often strapped into an appliance with a rod to straighten his back and a screw to hold his head, which often leaned to the right. As an adult Wilhelm hid his disability by holding gloves or a sword, as evidenced in photographs.

Wilhelm was sent away to school when he was sixteen and he wrote to his mother frequently. These letters revealed a desire for his mother to accept him as he was. Her letters in return talk about politics and art. His hatred for her began at this point and rapidly grew out of control. The doctor who delivered Wilhelm was English as was the doctor who treated his father during an unsuccessful battle with cancer. That doctor had misdiagnosed a tumour as benign. Wilhelm must have felt that both these had let him down and as they were English, like his mother, he aimed his hatred in that direction. 'One cannot have enough hatred for England,' he is reported to have said.

Even whilst he was in England with the rest of the family at the death bed of his grandmother in 1901, Wilhelm was building a fleet of battleships in the North Sea to challenge the Royal Navy. His grandmother died in his arms, boosting his claim that he was her favourite grandchild. His mother, Vicky, died from cancer a few months after his grandmother's death, severing any direct ties he had with England. Kaiser Wilhelm's rivalry with his cousins, coupled with a hatred for England was at least partially to blame for leading Europe into an unbelievably destructive four years.

Archduke Franz Ferdinand, whose death triggered the war, had many friends in England. He had visited in November 1913, several months before his assassination. The trip included time spent with the King and also with the Duke of Portland at Welbeck Abbey in Nottinghamshire. Britain going to war was not only a national tragedy but, for those who knew the Archduke and Duchess, it was a personal one too.

The death of the Archduke Franz Ferdinand resulted in the Austro-Hungarian Empire squaring up against Serbia. Germany supported the Empire and Russia stood firmly behind Serbia. This all happened in the month after the assassination of Franz Ferdinand in Sarajevo, although at this point it seemed largely posturing and positioning. It was not until 29 July that the Austrians bombarded Serbia. On 1 August Germany declared war on Russia and two days later on France. It was on that date, 3 August, that Britain ordered mobilisation of its own troops. Britain declared war when Austro-Hungary failed to comply with an ultimatum to respect Belgian neutrality. The date was 4 August 1914 and the time 11pm.

Immediate Reaction

The Nottingham Evening Post reported the next day that there had been an unprecedented call to arms. Men had flocked to join up; the ranks

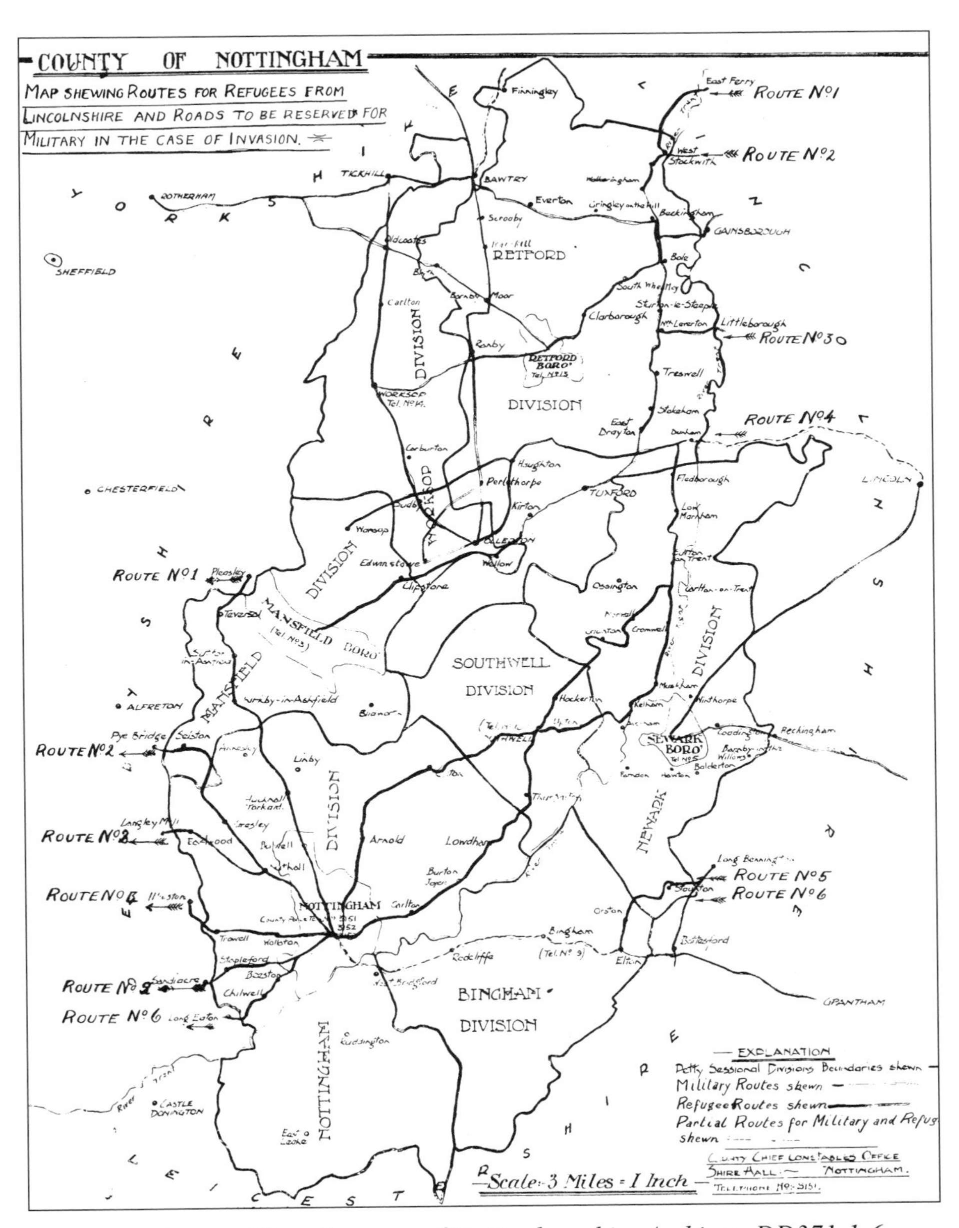

Escape Routes Plan. Courtesy of Nottinghamshire Archives. DD371-1-6

of the Robin Hoods and the South Nottinghamshire Hussars were billeted in the Albert Hall Institute; the Nottinghamshire Royal Horse Artillery were accommodated in the Notts County ground on Meadow Lane with the horses stabled nearby. Men continued to arrive in the City all day and kept themselves busy by collecting kit and getting ready to parade. It was said that every train passing through Victoria Station, once a bustling railway station, now a shopping centre, was stuffed full of khaki.

The rush to join up was accompanied by a rush in other services too. The General Post Office were quick to absolve themselves of any responsibility for late parcels and letters given that railway timetables would now be in disarray due to the movement of troops. Midland Trains cancelled all excursions and local services were cut back in order to provide trains for the movement of troops. The banks were closed and Nottingham's well to do were, declared the *Evening Post* on 6 August, buying up stocks of everything they could find. A special meeting of Nottingham Trades Council was held with the aim of persuading the Government to regulate food sales. This call went unheeded, as full rationing was not introduced until early 1918. Nottingham's knee jerk reaction was short lived and when the banks did open there was no run on funds.

The Empire and Dominion came to Britain's aid almost immediately. Canada gave a 'Splendid Gift' of one million bags of flour, each weighing 98lbs. This was promised in a telegram of 6 August to the government, with shipment expected to be within ten days. The responding telegram read, 'His Majesty's Government accept on behalf of the people of the United Kingdom, with deep gratitude, the splendid and welcome gift of flour from Canada.'

By the tenth of the month queues began to form; a sight that would become too familiar over the course of the war. This first queue was found outside the Nottingham War Relief Fund on South Parade, just off the Market Square. The queue was of women and children, described as anxious looking but patient. They were the wives of naval and military reservists who had already been called up and they were desperate for help. Their husbands had been sent off with three shillings, a few rations and a train ticket, often leaving their wives and

Signing Up. Courtesy of Nottingham City Council and www.picturethe past.org.uk. NTGM010905

children at home almost destitute. The fund was run by Mr A Durose and Mr HS Whitby, both of whom had run the South African War Fund. Some ten volunteers helped out. These women in the queue had to give details of their income, their dependants, their rent and any illnesses in the house. They would then be given coupons to take to tradesmen who would exchange them for goods of a certain value and who in turn presented the vouchers to the Fund for payment. Other equally practical matters were being organised. Sir Thomas Stanley Birkin of Ruddington Grange was the second Baronet, the title created in 1905 for his businessman father, Thomas Isaac Birkin, who was a lace manufacturer. Thomas Stanley offered to equip part of Ruddington Grange as a hospital. Fifteen beds and all the necessary surgical equipment would be provided. Nottingham's hospitals were also gearing up to receive the wounded. It was not known at that point whether our hospitals would be needed but Nottingham would be ready. Help was requested of local women to begin making garments for use by the wounded who were expected in Nottingham.

We also gave generously in the first ten days of the war. By 14 August the sum of £14,126 was raised in Nottingham. A list of donations was published daily in the *Post* with amounts ranging from £1 to £100. Donors included the local Lace Manufacturers' Association, £100; Nottingham's librarian Mr J Potter Briscoe, £5; and the Reverend Hodden gave £50.

Food

1914 provided a bumper harvest, the wheat crop being up ten per cent, and more raised cattle than any previous year, although by the end of August prices had risen, mostly by half a penny per pound for the basics. Butter was priced at one shilling and five pence per pound, margarine nine pence a pound and lump sugar four pence a pound.

One of the side effects of the war was the long queues and the lack of supply of certain goods. One Nottingham resident remembers that there were no ration books at this time.

'You used to stand in those 'ere queues and perhaps it got to you and there's nothing for you. "Sorry it's all gone," they'd say,' commented Ada Green. (1)

Goose Fair

Nottingham has a long tradition, over 700 years, of holding a fair in the first weekend in October. Goose Fair was originally a trade event for the selling of livestock and produce. It was also well known for its cheese. Today it is known for its scary rides and mushy peas. It was cancelled once before, in 1646, due to an outbreak of the bubonic plague, and at the beginning of September 1914 a decision was awaited on whether the fair would be cancelled for only the second time in its history. Opinion was divided as to whether it was right to hold the fair and be having fun when friends and relatives were risking their lives abroad. Local religious groups and traders, as well as the showmen, all made representations to a special City Council meeting to discuss the issue. Many would lose vital income, not just the showmen themselves but the businesses surrounding the Market

Goose Fair 1914. Courtesy of Nottingham City Council and www.picture thepast.org.uk. NTGM001513

Square where the fair was held. Reverend Grant stated that he was not opposed to the fair but thought that it was an insult to those serving for the fair to go ahead. A letter to Reverend Grant from Mr Weinberg, who had two sons at the front, said that it would be 'callous to go ahead when their relations and friends were being butchered wholesale'.

On the other hand, Reverend T Horne, chaplain to the Showmen's Guild, pointed out that 73,000 people made their living this way and that Nottingham did not want people to be continually dwelling on the horrors of war. The Council resolved, twenty-three for, seventeen against, with five abstentions, to hold the fair as usual.

Crime

The war also brought opportunities in various ways, not least to the less scrupulous amongst Nottingham's residents. Arthur Farley, aged twenty-six, from Gertrude Road West Bridgford, was arrested on 11

September in the Arboretum. He had ten forged £1 notes in his cap. A new £1 note had been issued in August. Farley led police to the bank of the River Trent, just below Colwick Hall, where a box containing a plate and a further forty-seven notes had been buried. The copies were said to be good but the watermark was absent, which is what gave him away.

The first of many cases against women was heard on 15 September 1914. Emma Oliver, of Martin Yard, Leenside and Maggie MacGuire of Dunnet's Yard, Thoresby Street were charged with obtaining money by false pretences. Oliver had claimed that she was dependent on a son who had enlisted and had another two children who needed feeding. In fact, her son had been called up but she was not dependent upon him. MacGuire claimed she needed food for her children when they were actually living with a relative. The women were sentenced to fourteen days in gaol each. The magistrates emphasised the seriousness of defrauding a charity.

Fundraising

Whenever something was asked of the people of Nottingham they gave as much as they could. An appeal in November for money to send boxes to Nottinghamshire soldiers containing chocolate, plum puddings, tobacco, mittens and other items was answered with enthusiasm.

The girls from Boots used their knitting skills to make gloves, socks and scarves to send to HMS *Nottingham*. They sent so many that the Captain wrote to explain they had had to give some to other ships! The girls also sold their items outside Boots' Station Street offices to raise money for more wool to knit more items.

Rev H Gifford Oyston, of the Wesleyan Church in Nottingham, produced a book of pamphlets containing his sermons in 1914.(2) They moved from hopes of rapid peace to prayers for the safe keeping of our troops. In addition, he held several fund raising events. On 11 October 1914 an evening was held on behalf of the Belgian Relief Fund. A large number of Belgian refugees had found their way to Nottingham. Many people gave money and many more gave their time. Some of the donations were as follows:

• A house free of rent for six months;
• Domestic servants in a house in The Park, an exclusive residential area designed by TC Hine, gave seventeen shillings;
• Offers of services including decorating, plumbing, clerical, interpreting, sweep of a chimney at cost, groceries at wholesale, adoption of orphans, cleaning windows, house cleaning, soap for cleaning, brushes for cleaning, labour offered for a day and a half, sewing and nursing.

Spare items were donated, including six single beds, six bedspreads, one bedroom suite, one dining room suite, two cribs, thirty-eight chairs, four easy chairs, twenty-seven blankets, eighteen sheets, ten pictures, thirty pillow slips, six pillows, forty-eight knives and forks, twenty-four teaspoons, twelve tumblers, twelve cups and saucers, twelve plates and twenty-six towels.

Reverend Gifford Oyston, wrote 'People to whom sixpence is a real gift signed away shillings...The people could not restrain themselves and the relief came in clapping.' When Belgian refugees arrived in Nottingham they were met by members of his congregation at Victoria Railway station and taken to 124 Mansfield Road. The rent had been paid on this property for six months. Presents were given to help make the house a home and a meal was made for the lucky family. Close to 1,000 people had a part in making those particular refugees a home. At a welcome meeting of the church a few days afterwards the Belgian refugees sang the Belgian, French and British national anthems.

Business

Other problems did not disappear just because there was a war on. In September Nottingham Lace outworkers claimed to be underpaid by about one third. The Trade Boards Act had brought in minimum wages for lace workers, and so middlemen and women, responsible for paying the workers, were summoned to court to account for themselves. William Lowe and Harriet Alvey were fined five shillings each and ordered to pay the arrears to the outworkers.

Our local firms also played a large part in the local war effort. Boots topped up wages for the wives of their employees so that they would

Thomas Adams Dye House. Courtesy of Nottingham City Council and www.picturethepast.org.uk. NTGM003050

not be going short whilst their husbands were serving their country. Player's cigarettes were regularly sent to the front, by way of the Cigarette Fund, and letters were received from soldiers who claimed that their lives had been saved because of their smoking habit - an idea completely alien to everything we are told now.

Entertainment

As is usual for the British, we in Nottingham tried to keep life going as normal during a very difficult time. In September 1914 the *Pearl Girl* was playing at the Theatre Royal. It was described by the *Post* as a 'Rippling melodious score with several numbers of exceptional merit and a capital libretto by Captain Basil Hood'. According to the *Post*'s review the woodland scene was picturesque, there was an 'emporium' of pearls and Miss May Tomlinson was engaging as the heroine.

Meanwhile, at the Grand Theatre *A White Slave* was playing. The story was of the attempted theft of plans for a new gun and the saving of the situation by a plucky boy scout.

Duke of Portland

At the outbreak of war, Willie Fernie of Troon was laying out the golf course for the Duke of Portland at Welbeck Abbey. He and his two sons were at Welbeck when war was declared. Both sons enlisted and Troon found himself apologising to the Duke for the delay in finishing his golf course. The Duke seemed to suffer the inconvenience and took a very active part in the life of the City and County and helped raise a huge amount of money for war causes.

Women

A letter written on 23 October 1914 came from Nurse Whalley, Queen Alexandra's Imperial Military Nursing Service, No 11 Stationary Hospital, British Army Field Service.(4) She wrote 'I wish you could taste the Indian meal I have just seen cooking. The curry is a bit too hot for us Britishers. The goat too recently killed to appeal to our English taste.' She continued, 'We are under canvas as the above address will infer. The weather is perfect, the country around also. The world in general is beautiful. The state of things as far as man is concerned is lamentable.' And it would only get worse.

Amy Isabella Mary Mundy was an invalid spinster, aged thirty-six, living at Rose Cottage, Burton Joyce. She lived with her seventy-two year-old widowed mother, Mary Ann Blatherwick, and her brother, Albert Thomas Mundy, a fifty-three-year-old out of work butler, according to the 1911 Census. Amy kept a diary and although she did not write copious amounts her short notes conveyed the essence of her life and the effect the war had upon it.(5)

Her first war time entry was on 2 August, when the newspapers were full of talk of war. 'War, war, war,' she wrote, sounding like she was already fed up of the topic.

> August 9 – Battle fought. Miss Blagg came. A very funny day. War.
> August 11 – Went to the hospital. Territorials and horses all about the city. A never to be forgotten day. Went to see Agnes.
> August 12 – Home all day. Dr Allen went to the Front.
> It must have been strange for someone you knew to be sent

overseas to a war zone and although Amy does not reveal any feelings in her very matter of fact recordings, she must have wondered if he would return safely.
August 15 – Went to the Picture Palace on Long Row.
October 13 – Dr Allaway came. Mrs Johnson ill. Lovely weather all week.
October 23 - Mrs Johnson died. Also Uncle Alfred.
[Was there an epidemic of some kind? Were they old? Amy has left no clue.]
October 25 – Very foggy morning. Rained hard nearly all day. No one came.
October 28 – Sent some clothes for Belgians at Carlton.
October 30 – Started scarf for soldiers.
November 4 – Finished scarf.
[Although Amy's contribution to the war effort was not as great as the soldiers or the munitions workers, she nevertheless did her bit.]
November 15 – Snow fell.
December 18 – Ma took eight flags and little box to Miss Partridge for Belgian Fund.
December 25 – Went to church and then to the hospital in the evening (General Hospital) and chatted with the wounded.

Amy was clearly a lady of leisure. No money worries were discussed, no mention of work, lack of food or any of the issues that affected the lives of inner city women on a day to day basis at that time.

A meeting of the National Union of Women Workers was held on 2 October at 11 am in the Mikado cafe overlooking the Market Square.(6) Their discussions included:

Garments for Soldiers

Mrs Handford reported that the appeal for making garments for Nottinghamshire soldiers had received good support and already large consignments of goods had been sent to various battalions. Requests for the garments were coming every day and parcels were sent off direct to the troops at once as far as the supply allowed. Around £136 had already been received to be spent on materials and for providing work for the unemployed. A motion was carried for a helper to be employed at ten shillings a week.

Girls' unemployment
Miss Guilford thought something might be done by teaching girls to work the Hanlec lace machine and the secretary called attention to the new scheme for toy making in the city. Both of these matters would be brought to the notice of the Queen's Work for Women Committee.

Soldiers and Volunteers

Nottingham was quick to answer the call for volunteers. It was reported in the *Post* on 5 August, only one day after war was declared, parades

Foresters March. Courtesy of Nottingham City Council and www.picturethepast.org.uk. NTGM010937

had been held in Nottingham of volunteers for the Robin Hood battalion. Nottingham trams offered free rides for Territorials in uniform.

A letter from War Office London SW dated 7 August 1914 was sent to the Territorial Force Association for the County of Nottingham.[(7)] It read as follows:

'Sir,

In the present grave emergency the War Office looks with the utmost confidence to you for a continuance of the invaluable help which you have given in the past.

I therefore desire to invite your co-operation in the work of raising the additional number of regular troops required at once for the army.

It is intended to enlist as soon as possible 100,000 men and I would ask you to use your great local influence and that of the Territorial Associations to secure these necessary recruits as soon as possible.

The men will be accommodated in camps established at or near the existing regular depots to which intending recruits may be sent, the camp nearest the place from which they are drawn being selected.

No responsibility for clothing or equipping the men will devolve upon County Associations, this will be arranged by the military authorities.

Members of the Territorial Force may be enlisted provided they fulfil the prescribed conditions as to age and physical fitness.

Territorial Force units that are at full strength will not recruit additional men until the 100,000 men are provided but should any of their numbers desire to join the regular forces now being raised their places in the territorial unit should be filled as soon as possible by men desirous of joining the Territorial Force only and not the regular army.

Territorial units available for foreign service will naturally not be affected by this recruiting of regular troops.

Such is the general outline of this scheme in furtherance of which you are desired to cooperate as far as possible.

It is not an ordinary appeal from the army for recruits but the formation of a second army and it is hoped that you will be able to assist in getting the men in every way in your power.

I am, Sir, your obedient servant,

Kitchener'

A special meeting to discuss the letter was held on 28 August 1914, chaired by His Grace the Duke of Portland. Many prominent

Humorous Cartoon. Courtesy of A P Knighton and www.picturethepast.org.uk. DCHQ504621

Nottingham citizens were present, including: Colonel CH Seeley; Colonel Sir Lancelot Rolleston DSO, who served with the 3 Regiment Imperial Yeomanry in the Boer War and was wounded in the arm, Chairman of Nottinghamshire County Council and Nottingham Quarter Sessions; Lieutenant Colonel Sir Henry Mellish, Alderman of Nottinghamshire County Council; Lieutenant Colonel RL Birkin DSO also of 3 Battalion Imperial Yeomanry; Captain McGuire, recruiting officer for Nottingham; and finally the mayor and town clerk of Nottingham. Although the majority of these men had already served their country, they were happy to provide more of themselves in a semi military capacity, serving once more.

Other local men were quick to show their support for King and Country. It was reported that in August 1914 1,860 men from Nottingham had already enlisted. Many more would swiftly follow and by 23 November the *Post* declared that 8,500 men had enlisted from Nottingham in three months including the Mann family from Temperance Cottage, Dame Agnes Street, who gave their sons William,

Players tin that saved a man's life. Courtesy of Nottinghamshire Archives. DDPL 6-18-1

Frank, Jim, Fred, George, Percy, John and Ernest to the cause. It was an enormous contribution to the war effort and well before men were being compulsorily called up.

9443 Pte G Dowsell 2nd Welsh regiment, 17 Ward, North Staffs Infirmary, Hartshill, Stoke on Trent wrote 'I owe my life to a tin of tobacco.' It was a tin of Player's Navy Cut. The sniper's bullet passed through the tin carried in his coat pocket instead of slamming into his body. He wrote 'Please send my tin back. I am in hospital with a compound fracture of the leg.'[3] He wasn't the only man during the war whose life was saved because of his smoking, many more letters were written to Player's telling how their tins had saved soldiers' lives.

Family

There are some things that never change from generation to generation and century to century. Things we still complain about today were evident one hundred years ago. A letter was sent, dated 28 August 1914, to the Education Committee by the headmaster of Southward Council School. He complained at the 'filthy and obscene language' being used

Royal visit to Lacemakers. Courtesty of Roni Wilkinson.

in the park adjacent to the school. The Education Committee sent the letter to the Town Hall only for the town clerk to pass it on to the Watch Committee.

1914 brought many changes to the lives of the people of Nottingham. Families were separated, money became tight and food short. This would be only the beginning of four very difficult years, not only for the people of Nottingham but for the whole of the country.

CHAPTER 2

1915: Deepening Conflict

The war was not five months old when New Year arrived. The conflict was no longer confined to just foreign shores. January brought the Zeppelins to Britain's east coast and the following month German U-boats began a blockade of Britain, targeting all vessels in Britain's waters including those from neutral countries. In the spring time offensives it became apparent that our boys did not have enough shells and those they did have were often of poor quality.

At home the barrage of restrictions had begun. People tried to continue as normal whilst putting their energies into getting on with it and raising money for the troops. Births, marriages and deaths were unstoppable; accidents still happened; crimes were committed, including some that had not existed before the war; opportunities for women increased, including at a newly built munitions factory; new regulations led to new prosecutions; businesses folded; men and boys went to the front leaving women behind to cope as best they could.

Fundraising

Although times were hard, money was tight and food was becoming an issue, the people of Nottinghamshire gave generously as always. By mid 1915 Nottingham's fundraising efforts were in full swing. It was reported in the *Nottingham Evening Post* on 2 July that the Gas

Workers and General Labourers Union had invested £5,000 in the war loan from their central funds. As half of all local subscriptions went to central funds, Nottingham's members had done their bit too.

A cake sale was held at the Exchange Building, on 7 July, in the market square where £75 was raised before the sale had even started. The Duchess of Portland had been due to open the sale but was absent as the Marquis of Titchfield, her son, was home on leave. The Duchess of Newcastle sent forty-five cakes to the sale. I wonder how many of those she made herself!

The War Help Committee in London wrote to Nottingham's Comfort for Troops Fund asking how they filled their boxes and the average cost. They had heard that Nottingham's boxes arrived in particularly good condition and wanted to emulate this.

Other methods of fundraising in Nottingham included a street collection for military horses, a flower sale in aid of Dr Barnardo's – those at home in need could not be ignored – flag days for injured military horses, Belgian refugees, soldiers and sailors. Even the children made a contribution by making lavender bags to sell to raise money.

Two major fundraising campaigns were organised that year, the Cigarette Fund and the Christmas Fund. On 12 October the Cigarette Fund stood at £101.14s.9d after only ten days of fundraising. For every sixpence donated, fifty Roll Call cigarettes, made in Nottingham at John Player's, would be sent. Nothing was deducted from the fund for expenses and only local troops would benefit. On 16 October it was announced that 100,000 cigarettes could be sent to the front. Messrs Gent of Broad Street donated three days of gross takings to the fund – one day alone raised £2.2s, not an enormous amount of the total but every donation counted. A letter from the Front was printed in the *Post* on December 2. The soldier concerned, unnamed, said the cigarettes arrived just when they were needed.

The other major drive spurred on by both our local newspapers, the *Evening Post* and the *Guardian*, was the Christmas Fund. The target was £8,000 for gifts to be sent to our troops. £850 was donated on the first day, 18 October. Two days later £1,080 had been raised and by the end of October that figure had risen to £4,617. The Christmas fund was closed on 1 December, having raised £8,206.19s.10d. An extraordinary 30,000 gifts were sent to our troops and Major Robert Sherbrooke, 1 Battalion Sherwood Foresters, wrote to the *Post*. 'I have just returned from a few days leave to find 1,000 boxes of gifts from our friends in Nottingham for the men.' It must have been an amazingly touching feeling for the soldiers to know that they were in the thoughts of all those people back home. Fundraising efforts were only one way that Nottingham showed their warmth and generosity of spirit during the war.

Accidents

As well as losing loved ones at the Front, families lost loved ones at home as well. James Patrick Walsh, thirty-seven, of the Royal Horse Artillery, was killed in June when his horse bolted because he was riding it when he should have been leading it. A clap of thunder startled his horse and Walsh's foot became entangled in the halter rope, pulling him under the horse. His head was banged several times on the road in Nottingham as the horse bolted and he died within half an hour of reaching the hospital.

William Weston Pickard, fifty-eight, of Mapperley, was killed by a sentry patrolling near the railway station in Nottingham. Private Thomas Isherwood shouted 'Halt!' Pickard did not. Isherwood thought the man was carrying a gun and shot him. It was later discovered that Pickard had been carrying an umbrella and was deaf. As the news spread throughout the city the place of the shooting was visited by 'the curious and morbidly inclined', according to the *Post*.

One of the many children involved in accidents during the year was Robert Emery, aged seven, who died in a lift accident at the National and Provincial Bank in August. It was thought that the boy peered down the lift shaft whilst pressing the button to operate the lift when the lift came down on his head. In June George Holland, nine, drowned in Sneinton Baths. He was in the deep end of the pool despite not being able to swim very well. His friends searched for him but because the water was so dark they could not find him in time.

On 4 September a stampede of mules occurred in Nottingham. They were from the 34 Ammunition Column based at Wollaton Park and

Victoria Baths Sneinton. Courtesy of Nottingham City Council and www.picturethepast.org.uk. NTGM003627

were marching to the goods yard in The Meadows. As they crossed a rail bridge a train went underneath, startling them. The mules turned and ran back the way they had come. Four men were hurt although, luckily, no one was killed.

Some accidents are as common today as they were a hundred years ago. It makes you wonder sometimes if we have learned anything in the last century. These kinds of pointless deaths still occur on our streets today.

Leah Winstein, thirty-six, of Peas Hill Road tried to put out hot fat by throwing water on it. The fat spurted everywhere and she suffered serious burns.

A boy of seven was killed by a car on Arkwright Street as he was going to the shops. He ran out into its path from behind a tram. The driver could do nothing to avoid him on that November evening.

Fire was also quite common on our streets. In September the medicated sweet factory, on Island Street and belonging to Boots, caught fire. Approximately 170 girls made their way to safety 'without panic' reported the *Post*. Boots' own fire brigade began to extinguish the fire before being joined by the City Brigade. It took an hour to put out and considerable water damage was done to the building. December also brought fire to the first floor premises of a new building on Broad Marsh when an oil stove was knocked over. The property belonged to Messrs Haigh, clothing manufacturers. The building was saved but most of the stock was damaged either by fire or water.

Weather

Nottingham had its fair share of tragedy and sometimes the weather was the culprit, much as it is in many parts of Britain today.

In February the city was blotted out by fog. It was described as being no ordinary fog. In places it was white and in other places it was yellow. Trams, cars and horses all crawled along at a snail's pace.

The now world-renowned Trent Bridge cricket ground suffered from the March gales. Part of the stands adjacent to Fox Road were destroyed.

The summer did not seem to bring any destructive weather but by the time winter came round again, so did sharp frosts followed by thick fog, in December. This time the fog was so thick that a tram ran into the back of a lorry going uphill in Lenton. The tram sustained more damage than the lorry. The tramcar then picked up speed going downhill as the driver could not put the brake on. It kept going until it reached an empty car on Gregory Street, which brought it to a halt. Luckily there were only four people in the tram and only one, a young girl, was injured.

In late December a gale and heavy rain arrived. Shop windows were damaged, a tree was uprooted on Woodborough Road and numbers 39 and 41 Alfreton Road had their roofs torn off. No one was injured but it took some considerable time to clean up.

Children

Nottingham's children played their part in helping the war effort. But this did not stop them behaving like children!

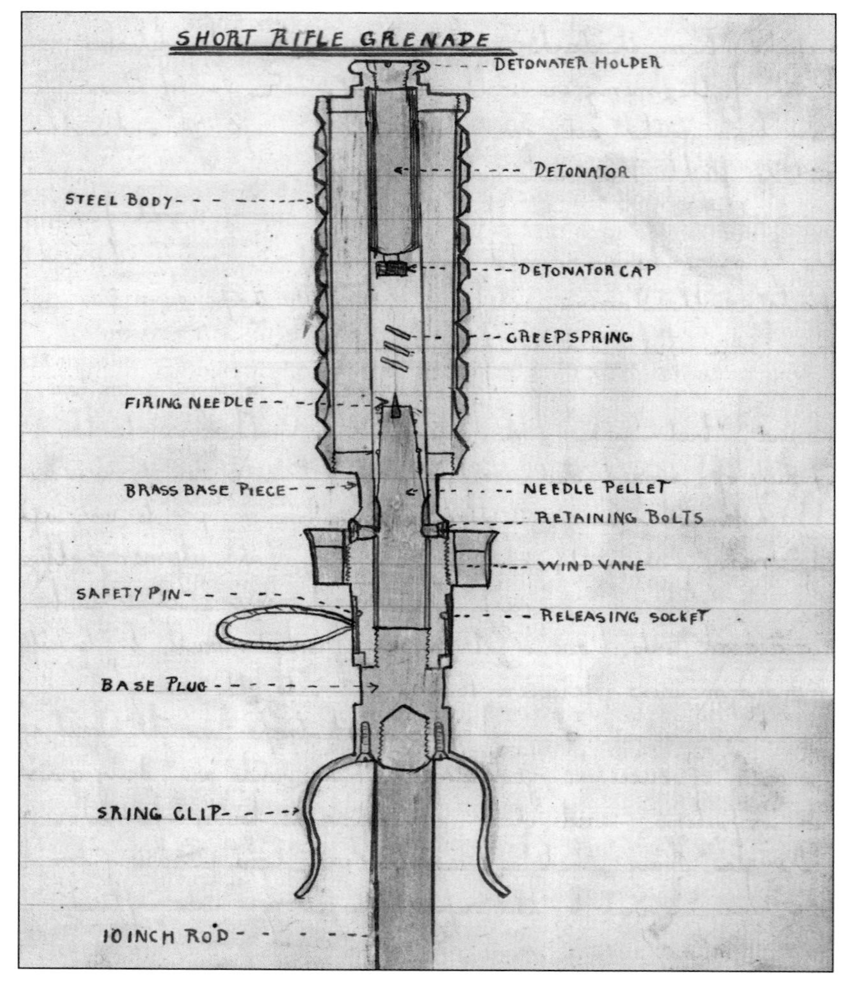

R Pegg's drawing of a grenade, aged 14. Courtesy of Nottinghamshire Archives. DD1280-2

In February farmers expressed their desire to use school children to replace their lost workers. It was a time when the farmers were being pushed to increase food production and with less people to help on the land this would be an almost impossible task. Children of thirteen, at a time when the school leaving age was fourteen, were allowed to work for farmers with the consent of their parents. A certificate of exemption from school would be given. If this was not enough, children between twelve and thirteen could be employed on the land temporarily, provided that they were only given work suitable for their age and physique. Girls would be given lighter tasks such as strawberry and pea picking. Some argued that this should be considered an extended school field trip.

However, not everyone was happy with this arrangement; the use of girls was opposed and farmers were described dragons! Others argued that teachers set school holidays to please themselves and school managers should be persuaded to give holidays at times to help farmers.

Children working in factories were protected by the Factory Act. Section 53 stated that anyone under sixteen should not be employed for more than seven days without being examined by the medical officer. Messrs Ashwell of Radford Road were fined five shillings for not complying with this rule in respect of two of their employees, as well as for not holding a proper register of under sixteens. The fine hardly seems worth the effort of a summons and certainly was not much of a deterrent.

Children were not only mistreated by businesses but sometimes by their own parents. In October, Gertrude Sheppard of 7 Davis Street was sent to gaol for two months for neglecting her children aged seven years and twenty-two months. When the police arrived at her house she was lying drunk on the sofa. There was no coal and no food in the house. But Gertrude was not the only one. Ethel Pike of St Bernard's Cottages, Querneby Road ill treated her eleven-year-old son and was given two months in gaol. He claimed she regularly attacked him with a broom. She also hit him across the face with a wet cloth. Dr Taylor said the child's body was covered in bruises and his face was swollen. His mother said she was not guilty and claimed that the boy had been fighting.

Not all children were little innocents. A special report from a Nottingham City Police Officer, Robert Abbott, dated 22 June 1915, stated that a number of boys had set fire to gorse on Bulwell Forest East golf links.[(1)] The complainant was George Wittlesea, the groundsman.

Eric Ludlow, assistant to George, told police that he had seen four boys amongst the gorse. He then saw the gorse on fire and the boys running off. Ludlow went after them and caught them in nearby Spring Lane. He took their names and addresses and then went back to help George Wittlesea put the fire out. Alec Parr, aged fifteen, from 2 Hazel Street, Bulwell, admitted finding a match then striking it and throwing it, setting fire to the hedge. He was with his two brothers and a few friends and they tried to stamp out the fire, found that they could not and ran off. The other boys were: Albert Burton, aged fifteen, from 57 Hazel Street; Alec's brothers, William Parr, aged ten, and George Parr, eight; and Ronald Thorpe, aged eleven, also from Hazel Street.

Bulwell Forest Park Committee received letters from the parents. Today you would expect them to be complaining of the treatment of their children but these letters show a different approach to parenting.

> 'I have received your letters with reference to my boys setting fire to gorse on Bulwell Forest. I wish to express my sincere regret at my boys' conduct and I wish to say that I have severely reprimanded them as to their future conduct, hoping for it to be overlooked this time.
> Yours respectfully, Private W Parr.'

Mr Burton was equally respectful of the authorities although his punishment of his sons seems to have been more severe.

> '57 Hazel Street Bulwell.
> I am very grateful to you for your letter with reference to my boy Albert Burton being associated with a party of boys who set fire to the gorse on Bulwell forest on 20 June. It has given me the opportunity of severely chastising him and also warning him against such conduct in the future. I regard it as a good kindness to me, his father, that more serious steps were not taken.
> Yours respectfully, William Henry Burton.'

Children also committed their fair share of more serious crimes too. In May four boys tied a cat to a post by the neck and then stoned it to death. Two of them claimed not to have taken part. The other two confessed to PC Horabin. The court fined the older two boys five shillings each and the younger two boys were cautioned. The court rued the fact that in children's court a thrashing could not be ordered.

Later in the year, a sixteen-year-old boy who operated a milk round for Allsebrooks, of Wollaton, was in court charged with embezzling. He took money from customers but did not hand it over to his employers. He wanted the money to go to New Zealand. He got as far as Southampton but could not get a boat so came home and made a confession. He was given two years probation.

Young people could be given strokes of the birch as punishment, if they were not heard in the children's court, although it did not seem to be a deterrent for some. Two boys aged twelve and thirteen stole shoes and took them to a pawn broker in Peas Hill Road. The broker took the boys to St Ann's police station as he did not believe the goods belonged to them. They were given six strokes each.

Half a dozen boys from Radford aged ten to fifteen trespassed on the railway at Wollaton. They played with the signals, tampered with coal trucks and then set off for the Wollaton Colliery Company coal yard. Once there they released a long line of trucks – some full of coal, emptied some fire buckets, put a signal at stop and threw stones at a cabin. The lads were charged with trespass and damage. The older boys were fined five shillings and the younger ones two shillings and sixpence.

The year ended on a positive note for children, however, with a pre-Christmas treat for 600 poor Nottingham children. The *Hippodrome* and the *Empire* raised money through collections and a football match to pay for a hot roast dinner and Christmas pudding. Tables were set up on a stage and the children were also given oranges, Christmas cards and a packet of sweets each.

Crime

Like all cities, Nottingham had its fair share of crime. Some was born of necessity, some of greed and some of downright stupidity.

James Fenney, alias Summers, was a soldier in trouble. He was charged with being drunk and disorderly, refusing to quit (meaning refusing to leave the pub), assaulting a landlord and damaging two decanters. Fenney was ejected from the *Crown and Anchor* in Sneinton Street as he arrived the worse for drink. Five minutes later he was back and he assaulted Mr H Peatfield, breaking the decanters in the process. Fenney apologised saying he was on sick leave from the army. He was sentenced to three months in gaol.

In May, the month a German U boat torpedoed the *Lusitania* and the Shell Crisis became known, Charles Fisher was fined twenty shillings or fourteen days in prison for fraudulently obtaining chocolate from a vending machine on Victoria Station. He had used washers instead of coins to pay for the goods.

Also that month Evelyn Mary Cooper, of Smith's Yard, Thoresby Street, was charged with attempting suicide by taking salts of lemon. She was described as a 'very low woman'. Annie Wilkinson, alias Bradshaw, was convicted of being drunk and disorderly in Canal Street. This was her thirty-ninth gaol sentence and she told the court exactly what she thought of them. 'I hope the Germans will come here and blow you all up before I come out.'

Thomas Blower, also the worse for drink, told magistrates that he would sign the pledge, if magistrates dealt with him leniently, until the war ended. He said he had had two rums, it being a hot day, that had upset him. It was his sixty-third appearance. His solicitor, HB Clayton, said he had appeared for Blower twenty-five times and he thought of him as an annuity. Blower was fined thirty shillings and signed the pledge, hoping that peace would come swiftly.

28 June brought the Quarter Sessions, the court system at the time for more serious crimes. That particular Quarter Sessions was the shortest one to that date, lasting a mere ninety minutes. The judge commented on the orderly state of the city and county, although if he had sat in the lower courts he might have had a different view.

Albert Doughty, twenty-four, of Newmarket Road, was arrested in Theatre Square, in July, for being cheeky. He made matters worse for himself on the way to the police station by throwing a police officer to the floor, ripping his trousers and biting his leg. He was sentenced to one month in gaol.

The evil drink struck again at the end of July when Elizabeth Dixon, alias Moore, appeared before the police court. When she left the employment of William Henry Brice items were noticed as missing. They included a gold watch, which she had pawned for £2. She was placed on probation and without a trace of irony in her voice gave her home address as Reform Terrace.

In August brothers-in-law Samuel Scrivens and Lawrence Wilkinson had an argument when the drunken Scrivens dug up potatoes from their shared allotment and threw them around. Scrivens was found guilty of wilfully damaging potatoes and issuing threats to Williamson. He was fined 10s or seven days in prison.

The lower courts saw many cases of soldiers and their mothers, or wives, being charged with making false representation to gain extra separation allowance. Four soldiers appeared on 14 September. They had over-stated their wages to ensure that their mothers received a higher allowance. They were John Burbage and his mother Mary; George Smith and his mother Elizabeth; JA Berridge and his mother Patty; and Arthur Whicher and his mother Betsy. There were many more cases of this kind during the war years. Most seemed to have arisen from misunderstandings of this new system although there were plenty who knew the system and tried to take advantage.

A few underage soldiers were caught out as they had to overestimate their income in order not to give away their true age. One such young man was Edward Inkley, of St Ann's Well Road. He and his mother were both fined.

Even the police did not avoid the embarrassment of the Court. PC Stebbing's wife appeared before a court on 17 August. The *Post* reported that Samuel William Blatherwick, bobbin and carriage hand a lodger of the Stebbings, at 108 Carlton Road, suffered a cut throat. It was thought at first that the wound was self inflicted. Shortly thereafter his landlady, Lillian May Armstrong Stebbing, was arrested for grievous bodily harm. Blatherwick was so seriously injured that his dying deposition had been taken. This case would not see a resolution until 1916.

The final word on crime should go to Frank Jammer Belshaw. His mouth had a way of running away with him. He was brought before the court on 15 September for verbally abusing a police officer who had tried to inspect his lodging house at 55 Red Lion Street. Whilst in the dock Belshaw had an altercation with Alderman Ball, father of Captain Albert Ball VC. Belshaw had served his country by digging trenches for a year before being invalided out. In court he pointed to the policemen and told them they should all go to the war. Alderman Ball stated that if the police did so the country would be left to the likes of Belshaw. 'Pity you didn't stay in France. You sound fit enough.' Belshaw was reported to respond that it was not his voice, it was his heart that was the problem. He also told the magistrates that they should enlist. 'It's you who treat us like dirty dogs that we have to go and fight for.' The case was adjourned to see if he could enlist again. His words would have struck a chord with many local people, given the inequalities that existed one hundred years ago.

Business

The war affected local businesses in many different ways. Some prospered, some struggled and some went bankrupt. All endured change.

Early in the year Debenhams advertised for 1,500 machinists for a new factory opening up on 8 March making women's wear, maids' wear and children's wear.

This was happening at the same time as the British offensive at Neuve Chapelle began. British losses amounted to 11,680 in three days. Some of the blame for its relative lack of success fell on the shortage of shells and artillery and the poor quality of those shells they did have. This led to the Shell Crisis and government action to tackle the issue of increasing shell production as quickly as they could.

In May it was announced that Cammell Laird were to build a munitions factory on King's Meadow Road. They also built one at Chilwell, providing several thousand jobs for mainly local workers. Cammell Laird designed, built and managed the factory without payment.

Some businesses suffered from strike action. In May the draymen walked out suddenly at J Shipstone and Sons Star Brewery in Basford. They returned to work two days later and continued their pay talks. It seems astonishing that some were arguing for more money when others were in life or death circumstances.

The lace trade were taken to task over wages paid to lace finishers. They were being underpaid but by the time the case came to court, Messrs Arthur Phelps and Wightman, the employers, had paid the arrears owed to their workers. The lace workers also claimed compensation from the Operative Lace Workers Society for injuries received due to the darkness of the streets. Three remarkably similar claims were made by individuals falling over and sustaining exactly the same kind of injuries.

Local businesses joined in the fundraising and also made their own efforts too. *Our Comrades in Khaki* was a magazine produced by Boots for their employees serving in the trenches. It gave news from home and even printed letters from soldiers at the front.

LEONINE ACHIEVEMENT.

AMONG the subscribers to the Prince of Wales' Fund, none is more constant than the marvellous Lion's Mane Postcard published by the firm. The lion depicted is not only a noble and spirited animal, but is also strongly gifted with acquisitiveness, and has already netted over eleven hundred pounds for the Fund. More than 600,000 presentments of that loyal mane have been sold, and from remote British Columbia to distant New Zealand his leonine highness is appreciated: and half the proceeds from the sale have been apportioned to the moneys graciously raised by our Prince.

Postcards 1d. each; 10d. per dozen; 10/- per gross post free.

Half the proceeds paid to the Prince of Wales' Fund.
:: On sale at all branches of Boots *The* Chemists. ::

War Seal Foundation

WAR DISABLED 1914-15 SERVICE SEAL ½d ½d

A meritorious plan for raising funds to help those disabled in the Empire's service is the War Seal Foundation. Everybody is urged to affix a halfpenny war seal upon all letters they post, and from the revenues thus derived, assistance will be given where it is greatly needed. Boots *The* Chemists have undertaken the sale of these seals at all their branches, and the entire proceeds will be devoted to the Foundation.

Back cover of Boot's magazine. Courtesy of Nottinghamshire Archives. DD2188-55

Volume One cost two pence and all the monies raised went to a fund for the sick and wounded. The complete cost of the magazine was borne by the company. A personal message from Jessie Boot and Lady Boot expressed their 'quiet and deep pride' in their employees. Lieutenant John C Boot, Jessie Boot's son, served in the 7 Battalion Sherwood Foresters and had many former colleagues from the company serving with him.

The bankruptcies of Nottingham's businesses showed no favour for profession, age or sex of the business owner. Bakers, lace manufacturers, fish sellers, grocers, builders' merchants, wine merchants and tailors alike were forced out of work by the down turn in trade. Of course there were others, such as William Calcutt, of 44 St Stephen's Road, Sneinton, who admitted that his business failure was due to his gambling.

Entertainment

'The show must go on' was the prevailing attitude and for the most part it did. Madame Fanny Moody appeared at the *Theatre Royal* in May, as the first Zeppelin raid on London killed seven and injured thirty-five, whilst George Formby and an 'exceptionally attractive company' were at the *Empire*. Miss Ellaline Terriss sang to the troops in hospital during her stay in Nottingham to appear at the *Empire* in July but after much argument in the Council Chamber, Goose Fair was suspended.

Family

Domestic troubles did not end with the onset of war. If anything differences became exaggerated as the pressure of everyday living increased.

Several divorces were reported in the *Post*, something that does not happen now unless there is a celebrity or something salacious involved. In June Emma Kinskind was brought before the court by her husband Charles for co-habiting with another man. When told he wanted a divorce the *Post* reported her response as being 'Thank God for that. I didn't think he'd do it.' Her lover, Thomas Pykett, asked the judge how soon he could marry her.

Food Production King Edward Park. Courtesy of Nottingham City Council and www.picturethepast.org.uk. NTGM010587

In December Harriet Bradley was granted a divorce. She was married in 1902 but James Bradley, a cab man, gave way to drink and abused his wife. His lover had also brought their child to Harriet's house, asking for money to support the child.

Families were under much pressure when husbands were overseas doing their duty.(2) Elizabeth Carr recalled, in 1984, how the war days had been for her. 'My mum had twenty-five shillings a week separation allowance. Our staple diet... was bread and dripping.'

Children were also having to grow up a little quicker, with 5,000 children throughout Britain having left school to work on farms by June 1915.

Aliens

There were quite a large number of German-born Nottingham citizens, most of which had not become naturalised. They turned up at the Guildhall on 14 May with all their belongings expecting to be sent away after registering. As it turned out the Home Office had not yet provided any instructions so they were all sent home!

Local feeling was vented against German business people who must have been friends with their neighbours just months earlier. The butchers' shops of Wagner in Hockley and Hoffman in Sneinton had their windows stoned. A woman and two youths were fined for the offence.

The story that shocked the locals was that of Alexander Seelig, a lace manufacturer of Heathcote Street, but residing in Radcliffe on Trent. He was a German who had lived in the UK for twenty-six years but had not become naturalised. Both he and his traveller, Resondo Villa Real, were charged with trading with the enemy. Seelig was interned and lost his business, which was valued at around £45,000.

Women

Although the war provided many hardships for women, with their husbands and sons off fighting, it also provided many of them with opportunities they could only have imagined before. The Duchess of Portland chaired a meeting early in the year that decided to extend the number of crèches available in the city so that married women could fill the jobs of the men at the front. Nottingham High School girls helped on the farm with weeding the wheat crop and Mr T Potter of Lambley provided accommodation and money towards expenses for a training course for women. Ten women were to go for two weeks to learn milking and light farm work.

In September, twenty women conductors were employed on the trams. The National Union of Women Workers, Nottingham Branch, received a letter from tram workers in Portsmouth asking them to outline how the women were employed. They replied that preference had been given to young women whose husbands were serving in the armed forces and as far as possible were from families of conductors who had gone to the front. The women worked ten hours a day and had one day a week off. They were paid the same as the men.

Three women were employed by the General Post Office at this time delivering mail in areas where there was ‘not too much walking’. Even women window cleaners appeared during this month. Six women were accompanied by one man, who carried the equipment and cleaned the upper floor windows of the commercial buildings they were working on.

Women appeared to be making great strides towards equality until you consider an advertisement published in December claiming to have

Tram conductress Donnelly. Courtesy of Nottingham City Council and www.picturethepast.org.uk. NTGM008413

the best Christmas present for the housewife – a triangular mop with an adjustable handle. Wow!

Many women went to work in the new munitions factory at Chilwell and earned themselves the name locally of the Canary Girls. The chemicals they filled the shells with, picric acid, turned their skin yellow. It was a tough place to work physically with the prospect of an explosion at any time playing on their nerves as well.

Amy Mundy's diary showed a different life to that of Nottingham's working women.[3] She lived in Burton Joyce and had no need to work.

> April 10 – Lovely Day. Alice Mee buried. Nell and I came [to her funeral] on her new bicycle.
> April 18 – Soldier F Walker came in am.
> June 7 – Very hot indeed.
> June 30 – Very severe thunderstorm. Kitchen flooded. 5 buckets and 3 baths full!
> August 1 – Very stormy, thunder and lightning.
> August 21 – Visit to Lowdham Grange [presumably before it became a young offenders institution!].
> September 8 – Me and Ma went to Beeston. Saw aeroplane.

Raleigh Munitions Girls. Courtesy of Nottinghamshire Archives. DD RN 6-2-1

September 17 – Made 24 bags for soldiers.
October 18 – Arthur's letter came from France.
October 30 – Inspector of Nurses came.
December 2 – Dense fog. Went to Joe's in afternoon.
December 6 – Sent parcel off to Arthur.

Although her entries are brief they still give a snapshot of her life at that time and of how little the war seemed to affect her.

Prosecutions

The introduction of many new regulations during the war led to even more bureaucracy to enforce these regulations. The second half of the year was extremely busy for the courts dealing with prosecutions under these new Acts. Most of these new rules covered lighting and food, with some early closing orders thrown in for a bit of variety.

Milk sellers were regularly fined for their product being deficient in fat; William Moss of Easthorpe Farm Ruddington was fined as was Ellen North of Randolph Street and Emma Johnson of Commercial Road, Bulwell. Farmer William Morris from Caythorpe was charged with watering down milk. He said he had provided the milk the way it came from the cow. His cows had only been fed on grass and hay although he was trying to improve their feed to improve their milk.

The lighting order provided the court with a considerable amount of work over the course of the year. Shopkeepers were fined including Fred Simpkins, butcher, of Goosegate; Henry Boul, confectioner, of Market Street; and licensee of the Rose of England on Mansfield Road, John Topham. Edith Phillips St Ives of Tattersall Drive was fined for not obscuring the light in the conservatory of her employer's house. Edith Bowne, her employer, was also fined twenty shillings.

Prosecutor JJ Williams asked the bench to impress upon the defendants the seriousness of their offence. A lighting regulations notice had been posted through every door but the number of cases steadily increased. The manager of the George Hotel, Sidney Leslie, was fined twenty shillings for not obscuring the library light and Mr Williams warned that in future the occupants of his rooms could also be fined.

Many landlords were fined for supplying beer after the 9pm deadline. Samuel Bacon of the New Inn Arnold was made to pay £3 in costs and was told to 'behave'.

As if these prosecutions were not enough, Nottingham police launched an operation to crack down on motor licences. At that time a motor licence had to be carried with the driver at all times. It was reported in June that fifty people had already been caught driving without a licence or with having a lapsed licence. One man had left his licence in France and another had emptied all his pockets at home before going to the recruiting office. It did not stop him being fined ten shillings. One man complained he had been stopped eight times in two days. On each occasion he had produced his licence. On the ninth occasion he could not find his licence even though he had it with him somewhere. He was fined anyway.

Volunteers and soldiers

Many Nottingham families gave men to the war but some gave far more than their fair share. Samuel Hardy, Hyson Green, formerly of the Royal Artillery, had seven sons serving and an eighth in the Metropolitan Police. Mr Hardy also had a son in law at the front and received a letter of thanks from the King's private secretary. HB Clayton, a local solicitor, had six sons at the front. That is a great deal for one family to give.

On 3 May *Nottingham Evening Post* announced that so far 25,000 recruits had come from the city and county, in a period of only nine months.

An advertisement was placed in June appealing for munitions volunteers. The graphic showed a working man with a sledge hammer flanked by a soldier and a sailor urging people to 'stand side by side with your military'. By 8 July nearly one thousand men had registered to be included.

A march organised by Nottingham and Nottinghamshire Recruiting Committee included an inspection of volunteer troops on the Forest by Lord Middleton on 10 July. Thousands had lined the route from its beginning at Wollaton Park Gates. The procession was headed by mounted police and the band from 152 Brigade Royal Field Artillery.

There were over 3,000 men in khaki including men from the Royal Field Artillery 34 Division Ammunition Column. The 3/7 (Robin Hood's) Sherwood Foresters; the Welbeck Rangers, the men of the Army Service Corps (Mechanical) and the Bantam Battalion of Sherwood Foresters. All of these men were training in the local area. It was hoped that the march would encourage others to join up. Several volunteers carried slogans of encouragement to those thinking of enlisting:

'Welbeck Rangers Fear No Dangers.'

'Robin Hoods Always Ready, Brave and Steady.'

The labour exchange was instructed to send men to the recruiting office, such as bricklayers and labourers for service in the Royal Engineers. These tactics worked and Nottingham men answered the call, with thousands of them rushing to join up by the end of the year.

The Rushcliffe Parliamentary Recruiting Committee discussed an unusual question: are bald headed men eligible to sign up or is it a reason for disqualification? As usual, local humour shone through. It

Drill Hall Derby Road. Courtesy of Nottingham City Council and www.picturethepast.org.uk. NTGM011058

Banner on Exchange Building Market Place. Courtesy of Nottingham City Council and www.picturethepast.org.uk. NTGM009119

was decided that bald headed men were eligible and if it came to it the man in question could 'throw his wig at the Germans to put them off'.

Of course, the more serious side to all these men volunteering was also seen in Nottingham. Many men returned to the city for care in our hospitals. They often arrived a hundred or 200 at a time, most savouring Nottingham hospitality for the first time, although some were our very own boys. On 4 May the wounded from the Second Battle of Ypres began to arrive whilst the contingent arriving on 29 September were said to still have mud on their boots from the trenches.

124 soldiers arrived on October 23; a further 142 just five days later and on 28 December 133 more arrived, including a man of seventy-one suffering from rheumatism. Most of the less serious ailments were Trench Foot, a painful condition brought about by standing in water at the bottom of the trenches for days on end.

Miscellaneous

The most shocking event of the year was the murder of British Nurse Edith Cavell. She was executed by a German firing squad for helping prisoners of war escape from Belgium to Holland. She saved many Allied lives and became a national heroine.

Apart from reporting the serious issues of the war the *Post* published the odd snippet of pure gold entertainment. A bullock running away from the cattle market caused excitement in the city centre on 16 June. It called at the Union Inn and, not having received a warm welcome, then made its way to Arkwright Street. Enticed by jam and sugar it entered the shop of Messrs Harrison. It passed through the shop, knocking over some jam, before charging up the stairs to the bathroom. The animal caught sight of itself in a mirror and stopped to admire the reflection. Drovers had now caught up with it which spooked the bull, making it turn and run down the stairs. It then ran onto Ryehill Street, London Road and back towards the cattle market. No one was hurt and the shop suffered minimal damage.

After a whole year at war the conflict had deepened and thoughts of a quick end to the war had dwindled to virtually nothing. The people of Nottingham had done their best in providing men and money for the war effort, something they would continue to do until the war finally ended.

CHAPTER 3

1916: The Realisation

The dawning of 1916 brought the realisation that the war would not end quickly. It was also the first war that was brought to Britain's shores. In addition to the U-boat and Zeppelin attacks of 1915 the first Zeppelin was shot down over Britain in this year by the Royal Flying Corps who used a combination of explosives and incendiary bullets.

In the Battle of Jutland on 31 May the German High Seas Fleet was forced back into harbour never to emerge again during the war until its very end, despite having caused significant losses to the Royal Navy with the loss of fourteen ships and 5,800 sailors. The second half of the year saw the beginning of the Battle of the Somme, a battle in four phases lasting for almost the rest of the year.

The country had a new Prime Minister in December when Herbert Asquith was replaced by David Lloyd George. On 12 December Germany delivered a peace note to the Allies suggesting a compromise.

At home compulsory enlistment was introduced by the Military Service Act and the people of Nottingham did their best to carry on as normal, coping with less food, dark nights and the growing influx to our hospitals of wounded men from the front.

Volunteers and soldiers

On 2 March the Military Service Act took effect. All men between eighteen and forty-one who had not yet attested (i.e. indicated preparedness to serve) were automatically part of the Army Reserves and the calling up of those men would begin within days.

Lord Derby's scheme was introduced in Nottingham. It gave training to attested men before they were actually called up and they were awarded with a certificate showing the training they had undertaken and the competency they had achieved. Men continued to sign up in droves and in May it was reported that Stanford Street recruiting office was as full as when the war had started almost two years before. Married men aged thirty-three to forty-one were expected to volunteer and Nottingham once more rose to the challenge.

Captain McGuire, Nottingham's senior recruiting officer was promoted to major in recognition of his excellent services. However, compulsory recruitment was not welcomed by every man in the city. William Prince, son of the landlord of the Greyhound Inn on London Road, had had a nervous breakdown in 1913. He had worked in his father's pub ever since. He went to Derby for his medical, expecting to be refused but he returned home in uniform. He drowned himself in the Trent shortly afterwards.

Other sons of the city achieved great honours. Captain Albert Ball DSO MC, son of Alderman Ball, was provided with the Freedom of the City for his heroic war record. Captain Ball gave the mayor photographs of himself in frames made from the propeller of a plane he had brought down in France. Unfortunately, he did not survive the war as he was killed in action in Spring 1917. He won a VC for services rendered between 25 April and 6 May 1917.

Disaster struck in August when HMS *Nottingham* was sunk by a U-Boat. Sir Ryland D Adkins commented on it during his Assizes session, which had only one case to consider. He said Nottingham had had to bear losses at the Somme and had now lost its ship although he was sure that the city would preserve its cheerful resolution and 'undeviating perseverance'. Thankfully most of the crew was saved and Captain Miller was given another ship in October.

Nottingham joined in a day of national mourning on 14 June for Lord Kitchener, who died aboard HMS *Hampshire* along with some 663 crew and members of his staff on 5 June. St Mary's churchyard in

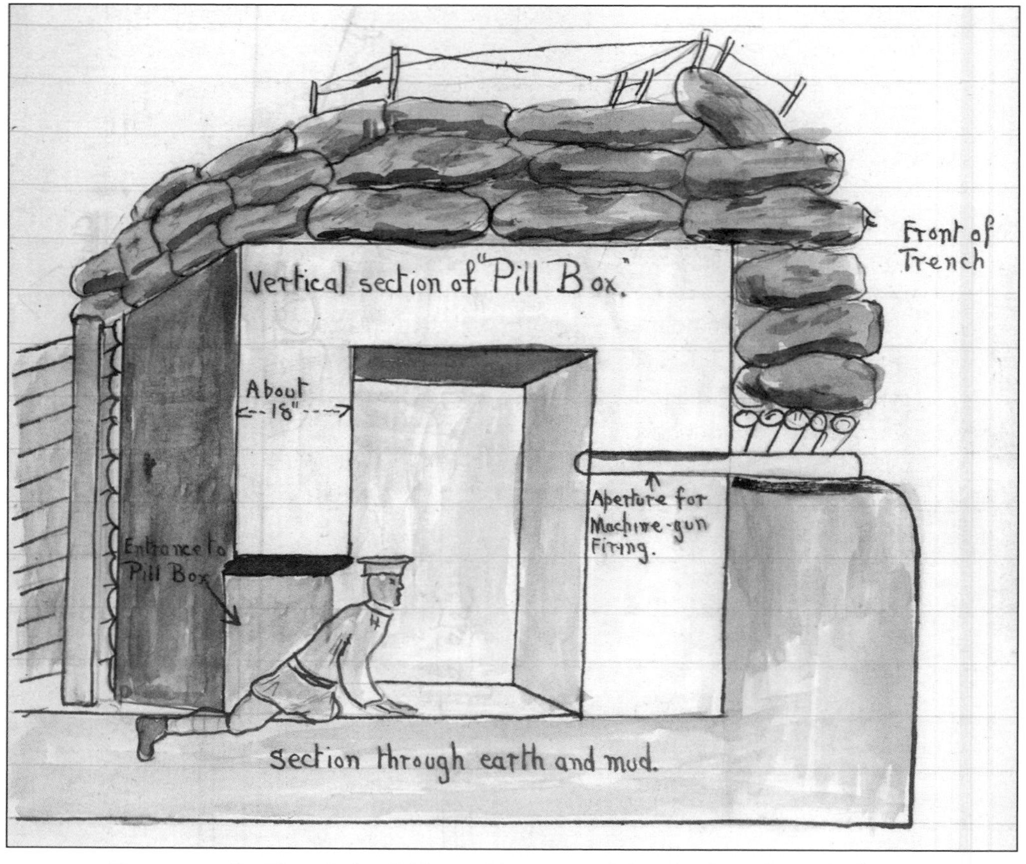

Diagram of a Trench by R Pegg. Courtesy of Nottinghamshire Archives. DD 1280-3

the Lace Market was crowded with local dignitaries, leading tradesmen, soldiers on leave and wounded soldiers for a service of remembrance. Kitchener died after HMS *Hampshire* was torpedoed off the Orkney Isles. Herkomer's portrait of Kitchener spent two weeks in the Exchange Building for people to view. Jack Cornwell day was celebrated in schools in September as the Somme offensive continued and tanks were used for the first time. Jack was awarded a posthumous

Victoria Cross for his part in the Battle of Jutland, when he remained at his post the only member of the gun crew still standing. The others were lying dead or wounded around him. He had several pieces of shrapnel in his chest and died in hospital shortly after docking at Immingham. He was just a boy aged 16½ when he died.

Many wounded men arrived in Nottingham following the start of the Battle of the Somme where seventeen British divisions deployed over a sixteen mile front. In one single day, 1 July, 60,000 men were killed, wounded or missing. They were met at railway stations by Red Cross vehicles, Special Constables and a fleet of private vehicles to convey them speedily to one of the many local hospitals. On 5 July 301 men arrived in Nottingham and on 7 July a further 200. Hospitals which received them included Bagthorpe, Musters Road, Carrington and Trent Bridge. Even the Albert Hall Institute was converted for use as a hospital, with the basement used as a dining room / recreation room.

Weather

On the first day of the year the temperature was recorded at 54 degrees, higher than some days in June 1915, when temperatures of 51 to 53 were recorded; in June 1916 the *Post* reported that those who had worked on Whitsun holiday had no grounds for disappointment as it was 7 degrees colder than Christmas!

The fog in November caused havoc when coupled with the lack of light. Alfred Oliver, a munitions worker, and Sarah Hazzeldine were both knocked down by tramcars, albeit in different parts of the city and Elsie Kenny, a twenty-four-year-old teacher, was killed at night in the fog by a bus.

Fundraising

Nottingham's generosity was tested again in 1916 and its people answered the challenge as usual.

Thank you letters were received from soldiers at the front for gifts of comfort boxes and cigarettes. Among the fundraising activities was a billiard game at the Grove Hotel, Daybrook for the Cigarette Fund. Landlord Mr Foster received several postcards thanking him. One was

Campion Brothers Motor Cycle Ambulances. Courtesy of Nottingham City Council and www.picturethepast.org.uk. NTGM008626

from boxer Corporal F Attenborough DCM. Foster had trained Attenborough for his matches.

A jumble sale was held by the Farmers' Red Cross fund. The aim was to raise £500,000 nationwide for the Red Cross, with Nottingham having its own target of £9,000.

The Cigarette Fund had raised £1,000 in just twenty-one weeks whilst subscriptions and a Flag Day paid for an ambulance, presented to the YMCA for their war work. Children's pageants and house to house collections raised money for YMCA huts, which were described as a home from home, to be placed at the front whilst flag days for wounded horses were all evident during this year.

The lace trade launched their appeal to raise £3,000 for ambulances to be sent to the front and a sale was held at the Mechanics Hall to raise money for clothing for the wounded in our local hospitals.

The Royal Ancient Order of Buffaloes presented their eighth ambulance car to the War Office on 2 October. They had already given three to the Red Cross, showing the men at the Front that they had not been forgotten at home.

In November the Christmas Comforts appeal began again. 4,000 men at the front were remembered with gifts. Nottinghamshire and Derbyshire teamed up to raise an estimated £40,000 within a month in order to get the gifts to the men in time for Christmas. The Duke of Portland, the Lord Lieutenant of Nottingham and a friend of the late Archduke Franz Ferdinand, led the campaign with his Derby counterpart, the Duke of Devonshire. 'We ask for the united, the hearty, the generous and above all the prompt support of both counties.' Which is exactly what they got.

On 9 October Captain Bayley of the Red Cross accepted seven ambulances on behalf of his organisation in a ceremony at the front of the Exchange. He spoke of the generous nature of the workers of Nottingham. In November a rest hut was erected at the top of Queen Street for use by soldiers who passed through Nottingham. It was made of brick and wood, could sleep thirty men and also had camp cots for another thirty men at night. Now that is a hut Nottingham-style!

Crime

Nottingham criminals had as equally a busy year as our fundraisers. Some were driven to crime by desperate need, some by greed and some by stupidity and laziness. The crimes themselves ranged from petty matters and crimes fuelled by drink to those of the most serious kind. The greed of George Rhodes, nineteen, and Harry Setchell, twenty-two, led to a conviction of theft for George and of receiving for Harry, whose front room was full of bags of oats and corn. Both charges were adjourned generally (meaning the court would do nothing further whilst they stayed out of trouble) on condition they signed up.

Frank Pepper was given the same treatment when he appeared in court after robbing famous vocalist Robert Radford. He stole £3 and his probation officer thought he could persuade the Merchant Navy to take him.

Being found drunk led to many court appearances for men and women alike starting in January and going right through until December.

Soldiers faced danger away from the front line too. Charles Moore refused to leave the Peacock Inn during a night out in January and threw a brick through the window when he was forcibly ejected. He drew a knife on two soldiers who went to capture him. He had previously been convicted thirty-five times (including eight for assault) and was jailed for four months.

Arthur McCoy, aged forty-three, was charged with being drunk and assaulting PC Hubbard. McCoy was one of a group of twenty-six men who turned up for work at the munitions factory whilst drunk.

Two sets of handcuffs were used on Walter Adderley as he was removed from the Grove Hotel on Castle Boulevard. He drunkenly assaulted Sergeant Clarke. Constance Welbourne took the collection box from the Dog and Gun in Trinity Square whilst she was under the influence of drink. She was given probation after her husband pleaded for her.

By August the chairman of the Magistrates Bench was fed up and decided to make a comment on this situation. 'We have sat here three times this week and it is nothing but drunken cases. Something ought to be done to remedy this state.'

Unfortunately no one took any notice of his plea and soon after Lucy Donkersley was fined for allowing drink to be consumed during prohibited hours at the Railway Inn on Station Street. She had given the beer to a non-commissioned officer resident at the Inn.

John Pears of the Enterprise Hotel on Woodborough Road was fined ten shillings for selling whisky. His solicitor complained of the way these types of offences were brought. Officers were sent in to ask for whisky and were therefore also committing an offence. One officer was said to have had at least five whiskies before telling the landlord he was a police officer!

Some soldiers tried to help, as in the case of Charles Moore, but others were the instigators. A wounded Nottingham soldier, unnamed, was charged with being drunk and disorderly and wilfully damaging a glass panel at the Swan Hotel. He was fined twenty shillings but the landlord paid this for him.

Private Betts became a victim when he was assaulted by Naomi Smith after refusing to give her money. Naomi was imprisoned for one month, though she stated that she could do the time 'standing on her head'. Clearly not her first offence.

Many cases of neglect were brought to the courts also. Some women had not been able to cope whilst their husbands were away at war. Other women had lost interest in their children. At a time when there was no contraception, life was hard and the number of children in a family was often large, it is perhaps understandable although not condonable.

Mary Ann Huthwaite was sent to gaol for one month. Her eldest two children were on probation, neighbours said she was never sober at weekends and the home was squalid. Her 'husband', Robert Laurie, was told to sort it out whilst she was resting in gaol.

The more serious crimes of the year involved a robbery at a jewellers, a counterfeiting operation and a murder charge.

Butcher and Swann were the jewellers who suffered at the hands of John Grey, a cycle fitter, who had been convicted of receiving stolen goods. The counterfeiters were caught when one of the two women involved, Gertrude Friend, passed a florin off as genuine in a shop. The fake florins were lighter than the real thing and had been made with different metals.

In June Ernest Middleton was charged with the murder of Ida Sinclair by 'unlawful operation'. She later died. He carried on his business under the name of Dr De Boi, although he was not a doctor. He received seven years penal servitude. The newspaper report provided no details of the 'unlawful operation' but the author can only assume it was an abortion. This was clearly not an easy time to be a woman.

There were also lighter moments in court. Henry Ernest and Frederick Leaper were fined for stealing 200 cabbages from an allotment, petty acts at a time when our troops were risking their lives in the Battle of the Somme. Sixty-one year old Annie Hodder was in court again for stealing sheets and clothing and pawning them. She had committed this offence so often it had become known as Hodder's Hobby.

Munitions

The munitions tribunal sat regularly to hear and decide upon any munitions matters that arose, except for the men that brought matches into work who were dealt with by the criminal courts. The tribunal would hear applications from men who wished to leave their current employment for other munitions work. Many of these applications were refused. Harry Bowles wanted to move to a factory nearer to his family. His wife and mother had died and he was struggling to care for his children. His employer said he was essential in building machinery for the hosiery trade engaged on Government work. Bowles' application was denied. Men who applied for a discharge certificate on the grounds that they could earn more money elsewhere came away disappointed. The munitions tribunal also operated as a disciplinary body for munitions workers. A total of sixteen labourers appeared before the tribunal charged with absenting themselves from work. They claimed their wages had not gone up in line with local trade increases. They refused to work until their wages were increased. The tribunal refused to order their wages to be increased but offered to refer them to arbitration if they went back to work.

James Lockley was fined £2 for missing a total of fourteen and a half hours work in the previous eighteen weeks and George Butler was tried for taking a bottle of whisky into the factory and being drunk at nine in the morning.

Entertainment

The year opened to *Little Miss Muffett* at the *Theatre Royal* with Marriott Edgar playing the Queen. The *Post* described the performance as full of 'mirthful points'. The mood was not so upbeat at the end of that month when Parliament passed the Military Service Act on 24 January, although this did not come into effect until 25 May.

Only a few months later the government implemented the Entertainment Tax and consequently a meeting of picture house managers was convened at *The Scala*. They were worried that the tax would mean the difference between a profit and a loss. It was decided that the whole of the tax would have to be handed on to the public. At the end of the year there was no pantomime at the *Theatre Royal* for only the second time in its fifty year history. This lack of entertainment was blamed on the scarcity of comedians. It was decided that a revue would be performed instead.

Victoria Embankment. Courtesy of Nottinghamshire County Council and www.picturethepast.org.uk. NCCS002474

The *Grand Theatre* did manage a pantomime that year, *Dick Whittington*. However, the principal boy and the dame were both played by women, something that is commonplace now, as men were in short supply.

Women

As in the previous year, women took up the slack wherever they could, although it was apparent that for some women the war was merely an inconvenience to their social life.

The Education Committee proposed that courses in business should be offered to women in order to fill in the gaps left by men who had joined up. Classes would include business arithmetic, correspondence, shorthand and typing.

The Munitions Committee overseeing the health of workers issued two statements. They said that it was undesirable for women to work at night, although they accepted its inevitability. They also said a three shift system should be implemented and that transport to and from work should be considered to keep the women safe.

Spring of 1916 saw the appearance of Nottingham's first lady taxi driver, Miss Alice Astill. She was soon to be joined by other women. She was paid the trade union rate of wages and commission, the same as the men. Miss Astill was formerly a shorthand typist and was an experienced driver.

Training centres sprang up in Nottinghamshire for women's agricultural courses. The main training centre was in Colston Bassett. It cost £14 per week to run, which was partly covered by farmers providing meals for the girls and paying money to the training centre for each girl who worked on their farm. The *Nottingham Post* carried a picture of the girls at work.

The National Union of Women Workers held a conference at the Mikado Café in September. During the meeting it was stated that many opportunities had arisen for women and their employment would show employers how much they had lost in not employing women before. Mrs Handford, President of the Nottingham Branch, commented that the British nation drank the value of a super dreadnought every five days. The author is not sure what evidence she based this on but it is surmised that she was a tee-totaller!

The Ministry of Munitions announced in November that women's war wages should be the same as men's if they were doing a man's job, which would be an average of £1 for a 48 hour week.

Our Nottingham women were recognised by the Welsh when Nottingham Girls Choir won the coveted Premier Honours at the Royal Welsh Eisteddfod. The adjudicator described them as having 'plenty of training, intonation and elasticity'.

For those women who did not have to work life was quite different. Amy Mundy wrote [(1)]

> January 1 – Terribly windy day. Afraid to go out. [Girls in factories and shops would not have a choice and would have to endure any weather to get to work.]
> January 11 – Lost my voice.
> January 31 – Two officers came. Visit of the Zeppelin, seen over Crow Park. Nottinghamshire in darkness. Damage in Derbyshire and Lincolnshire.
> February 3 – All talk was of Zeppelin raids.
> February 10 – Blower went off. We were rather terrified. No damage.
> March 14 – Went to sewing meeting.
> May 17 – Very hot all day. Balloon and 2 aeroplanes passed over here.
> May 24 – Empire Day. Lovely all day. Nurse Parry married to JW Ainsworth. Made the Union Jack yesterday.
> May 26 – Aeroplane landed for petrol
> June 6 – Nice day. News of HMS Hampshire and Lord Kitchener and General Staff gone down. Either mined or torpedoed. Calamity. [Although her descriptions are brief they are at least accurate.]
> May 14 –Sewed all day.
> July 5 – Very nice day. 301 wounded came to Notts. [The juxtapositioning of her phrases suggests a meaning different to that probably intended!]
> July 10 – 2 Aeroplanes passed over Burton Joyce.
> July 15 – Went to Skegness
> July 29 – Came home.

September 2 – Air raids at Retford and Cuckney.
September 18 – Made plum jam. 25lbs.
September 30 – George Jackson killed.
October 14 – Quiet day. Reggie Blatherwick killed.
December 3 – Very ill, went to bed.
There is no emotion in Amy's diary and little detail.

Amy's comments about the weather sometimes clash horribly with other comments on the same day. See 5 July for example.

Weather

The year started with reports of a 'seismic disturbance' at around 7.30 on the evening of 15 January. The *Post* then went on to say that hardly anyone noticed it and although furniture and crockery rattled no damage was done.

In February snow caused havoc with the trams and several telephone lines came down, isolating the city for two days. A shortage of horses and labour due to the war meant the City Council could not clear the roads quickly enough. Trees collapsed under the weight of snow on their branches and a man was hit on the head by spouting brought down by the snow. He later died in hospital. At the end of March Nottingham became isolated again as more phone lines came down. A gale force wind added to the problems and trains were hours late. Direct communication with London was restored on March 31 after a gap of three days.

Business

The year started with concerns about the shortage of lace workers now available. The *Post* reported that a 'twist hand was now having to do his own work'. Prior to this a twist hand would have another worker with him to help.

By July such issues were overshadowed by the plain net makers agreeing to strike over bonus payments. They did not receive bonus payments on all the goods that they made and strike notices were issued to their employer. Messrs Hicking (Lace Makers) was charged with breaching the Factories Act by employing women after 7pm. A factory inspector found several women working the 7pm – 7am shift. The court refused to register a conviction, stating that it was in the national interest to have workers around the clock at that time.

Although there were disputes between employers and employees, they generally stood together for the good of the war effort. Many firms worked during the Whitsuntide holiday in order to keep up production.

The War Office decided to release 1,000 attested men nationally to work in a municipal capacity. Nottingham used its allocation of men to remove rubbish, a welfare issue identified by the Medical Officer of Health for Nottingham Dr Boobbyer.

In February, Mason Brothers, bakers, had a fire at their premises on the corner of Russell Street and Tennyson Street. The firms' horses, stabled next to the bakery, were led to safety. Mason Brothers was not insured for the loss of a large quantity of flour, damage to the ground floor and the loss of the upper storey. The loss was estimated at £400 –£500.

Accidents

Deaths at the Front were not the only grief endured by Nottingham's population. The accidents suffered by local people were little different to those endured today. There were car accidents, tram accidents, gas poisoning (more commonly carbon monoxide poisoning these days), accidents involving fire and the curse of the useless fireguard.

In the first month of this New Year four motor accidents occurred in just one weekend. Injuries sustained ranged from bruises to a broken leg and the death of a five-year-old boy.

Tramcars were involved in many of the accidents that happened that year. In February a tram travelling from Carlton to Nottingham caught fire as wires fused. The conductor quickly put it out and within fifteen minutes the tram was on its way again with no injuries having been sustained by the passengers.

Those travelling in a tram in Sherwood Rise were not so lucky. Sixteen people were 'more or less' injured as the car sped down the hill out of control. It crashed into the car coming up the hill, with glass and wood going everywhere. Ernest Mills, driver, suffered a broken leg. The road was blocked for an hour.

A home brewery lorry and a tram car collided at Radford in August, leaving the lorry driver seriously injured in hospital. Apparently there had been some confusion over who had the right of way.

In the dark, street light free, nights of December, when the Battle of Verdun finally drew to a close after ten months, Mary Tainton, fifty-seven, of Brewers Yard was knocked down and killed by a tram car. The fact that she was deaf and suffered from poor sight had contributed to her death.

The year ended with two people being killed as a runaway tramcar collided with a stationary one in the Market Place. The runaway tramcar struck the stationary one broadside, knocking it over. Neither of the deceased were passengers or staff of the tram, the unfortunate two people being customers waiting for the tram to arrive.

Aside from fires at business premises in 1916, such as the several suffered by Boots on its Island Street premises, inadequate fire safety at home caused problems for many families. Arthur Wheelhouse, aged five, was in his house one October morning with his older brother when their mother had gone to work. He poked a stick through the fireguard into the fire. When he brought it out again his shirt caught fire. A neighbour rolled him in a rug but the child died in hospital. In December the coroner issued another warning to families as another child, aged seventeen months, died as a result of a faulty fireguard.

A woman and two of her children died at their home on Berridge Road West in July of gas poisoning. The woman's father came to visit and could not gain entry. He broke a window and smelled gas. The two children were found in bed alongside their mother, all beyond help. A third child was unconscious and rushed to hospital. A gas pipe in the bedroom was found to be leaking. At the inquest it was discovered not to be an accident after all. One of the children was found face down with a bonnet pushed into his mouth. Verdict: murder suicide. Imagine her poor husband's desolation on being told that his wife had killed his children and then herself. He was serving in the Royal Field Artillery.

Restrictions

Many new restrictions were brought in during 1916. January brought a new Lighting Order, with stricter controls. It also made allusion to railway sidings, which had previously been outside the scope of the regulations.

Further restrictions appeared in September. The Defence of the Realm Act brought in limitations on the hours that liquor could be sold. Landlords were worried about the effect that this would have on their businesses, especially those close to factories with shift workers.

Shops had to be closed by 7pm from October, due mainly to the lighting restrictions and fuel economy measures. There were various exemptions for shops that sold freshly cooked food, one of the excuses that would be used as a defence in the Courts when prosecutions were brought.

These restrictions brought a flurry of complaints to the City Council from the various local trades association, each complaining about others breaking the rules. Specifically, letters came from the Nottingham Drapers' Association, the Pork Butchers' Association, the Retail Confectioners' Association and the Nottingham and District Butchers' Association.

Prosecutions

New restrictions inevitably brought new prosecutions. Bureaucracy trundled on day after day in true British style as men lost their lives far from home and without the comfort of loved ones. Most of the prosecutions brought under the Lighting Regulations were due to carelessness, a fact that began to irritate the magistrates dealing with these offences. Several times they commented on this and vented their frustration at the lack of more severe punishments, especially for repeat offenders.

The year began with fines for John Marriott, an ironmonger, and Francis and Helen Everard Jackson, butchers. Marriott was said to be emitting enough light to read a newspaper by and was fined forty shillings. The Jacksons were fined twenty shillings.

Notices of the new regulations had been out since 15 December 1915, giving plenty of warning, in the opinion of the authorities, for people to get it right. The court's opinion was that defendants were either criminally negligent or absolutely defiant of the law. The defendants had a different view. They complained that it was difficult to know what the law wanted. Sir Thomas Birkin's lace factory at New Basford had 500 windows. Thirty were not covered, it was claimed, due to a lack of materials. A fine was still imposed. Mr Ross, a hosiery manufacturer, had covered the front of the property but not the back as he did not think it was necessary. He was also fined. Fifty-one summons were heard on that day, 16 February.

Less than two weeks later another fifty lighting summons were heard, most of which involved factories or shops. One defence stated that as they were doing war work the regulations did not apply. Apparently the Germans in their Zeppelins, which had come over our city in January of that year, could not see war work factories from the air! The legislation must have been poorly drafted to render that much confusion.

Even the General Post Office did not escape. Out of 880 windows in their offices on King Street, two let light into the street and it was fined. There was no exception either for houses of God, as the Wellyn Chapel in New Basford was fined forty shillings in March for twelve lights left shining. When Herbert Morley, a factory owner in Sherwood Street, complained of a £5 fine, the chairman said that if his own brother were before him he would fine him £10. He proved his point when magistrates clerk Mr T Cartwright was fined £2 when brought before the bench in May. At the same hearing the wardens of Holy Trinity Church were fined. They stated that the problem was that their windows had been cleaned and now let light out!

Mr F Acton, a local solicitor, told the court that the only safeguard from the murderers in the sky was complete darkness, a fact that seemed difficult for Nottingham's population to take in. The prosecutions and fines kept coming – by May £400 had been levied in lighting offence prosecutions. These offences were not the only ones raising money through fines. Albert Brookes of Kirkwhite Street was charged with speeding at twenty miles an hour. He claimed his motorcycle could not possibly go that fast.

Two unnamed men were fined, in May, for having no lights on their bicycles after dark. Presumably Germans were blind to these? One of the men, who did not appear in court, sent a letter from his mother asking to be excused as it was his first time out after dark.

Liquor also proved costly for Nottingham's residents. In October the first batch of summons was heard under the new liquor prohibitions with the offences of treating (buying someone else a drink) and selling or consuming alcohol during prohibited hours. The cut-off time was 9.30pm, with customers and publicans alike being fined. All were charged twenty shillings.

The Appeals Tribunal Court was kept equally as busy. Applications for exemption from call up were being made by employers and employees alike. Mr H Leman, solicitor, applied for an exemption for his two clerks saying that shorthand typists could not take the place of his clerks as their writing was not good enough. He added that schools were not 'teaching it properly now'. One appeal was dismissed and the other clerk was given a two month exemption after which he was expected to enlist.

The tribunal happily refused the appeals in most of their cases, as reported in the *Post*, although they did grant timed exemptions to Turner Brothers, which had a factory adjacent to Trent Bridge (now apartments). They had lost fifty-eight per cent of their workforce to the war. Griffin and Spalding were allowed, in March, to delay the call up of their one remaining man until June so that he could finish his apprenticeship.

The tribunal had very little time for men of conscience who objected to fighting. This author did not find one case where exemption was granted on these grounds. In fact most of them were handed straight to the military, who maintained a constant presence in court. Mr Rothera defending a conscientious objector in May commented on the lack of success in these cases. Mr F Acton on the bench stated that he had no discretion in these cases and that he had been surprised by the wonderful growth of conscience in the last few months.

Mr F Bolson appeared before the bench in March. He stated that he was happy to make shells but not to fight. 'It is a peculiar antipathy you have to taking someone's blood, is it?' He was then asked if he would allow someone else to take blood on his behalf. He sealed his own fate when he replied in the affirmative and his appeal was refused.

The tribunal often heard thirty cases in one sitting. A farmer with no workers left to help him, a builder who would go out of business if he was called up, putting the livelihood of ten men at risk, all appeared in one morning. The reasons for exemptions were sometimes valid, sometimes incredible but never dull or successful come to that. Walter Hooten, solicitor, claimed his exemption due to professional privilege. Appeal dismissed.

Sydney Herman Hempel appealed that his mother was English and his father was German and that he would fight for England as long as it was not against Germany. Appeal dismissed. John Bloom appealed on the basis that he was American, stating that he was born in Boston and his parents still lived there. It transpired that he was born in England and did not travel to the United States until he was 15. He had never become a naturalised American citizen. Appeal dismissed.

Messrs Peach and Co applied for an exemption for their book keeper. They stated that they had tried women in this role but it was just too complicated for them. My, my Mr Peach! Appeal dismissed.

In December Nottingham's *Theatre Royal* was raided and three cast members were brought before the court the next morning. All were handed to the military.

The presence of the military in court was used proactively, and possibly provocatively, in September. When the appeals had been heard and dismissed and the appellants handed to the military, the doors of the court were closed and locked, preventing the public from leaving. Each of the male spectators of military age in court was questioned as to why they were not serving. Two were detained pending the production of documentation. No-one in Nottingham was allowed to escape serving.

Children and education

Children's welfare came increasingly under scrutiny during this time, highlighted perhaps by their treatment in war time conditions. Not only were they working on the land and in factories, they were also being neglected and abused. Some things have changed for the better in the last hundred years, others sadly not. At a meeting of the NSPCC in the Exchange those assembled commented on how children should be nurtured and on the shocking number of cases of child neglect brought before the court. As a direct result, 'life guards' were placed on city trams and had saved the lives of five children in just three weeks.

Children's education was under review as well. The authorities were concerned at how much had been missed by those children who were working on the land. The Board of Education in Nottingham resolved to support their counter parts in Kent, who advocated that those children should be returned to education after the war.

At the Head Teachers' conference in June it was suggested that class sizes of sixty pupils were far too big and were no use to either pupil or teacher. It was also stated that the school leaving age should be raised to sixteen, which was something that didn't happen until long after the Second World War. The cost of these changes was said to be roughly equivalent to the cost of war for fifteen days. The government clearly had other priorities, given the length of time taken to introduce change.

Miscellaneous

The cost of the war was not often discussed in the pages of the *Nottingham Evening Post*, although when it did so the figures were astounding. In January the cost per year was stated to be £1,800,000,000. Herbert Samuel, in an address to the London School of Economics, stated that just as his generation had been paying for the Napoleonic wars, so would his children, grandchildren and even great grandchildren would be paying for this war.

At Nottingham licensing court on 9 March, liquor licences were transferred and renewed. Applications by the White Swan, Green Dragon and the Royal Marine were accompanied by complaints and the applications were adjourned for further investigation. Apparently drunken people had been seen leaving the premises.

Just before midnight, in the middle of March, a Special Constable and a clergyman were walking along the street. They saw something round, about the size of a football, fall onto the pavement and give off sparks. They thought it was a bomb and ran to the police station to get help. When they went back they could not find it anywhere. It transpired that a medical man living on Lenton Boulevard shut his gate so hard that the heavy stone ball on one of the posts beside his gate fell off and crashed to the ground hitting him on the way down. As soon as he had recovered a little he picked the stone up and put it back, not realising the excitement it had caused.

On the night of Saturday 23 September nine Zeppelins flew a bombing mission over England. One of them found its way to Nottingham. It dropped devices in the Trent, just north of Muskham, passed Southwell at 12.15 am and Gunthorpe at 12.23 am. Six bombs aimed at the lit up Colwick sidings fell into nearby fields. Six more bombs fell on fields between Colwick and Sneinton. Other bombs damaged a chapel, partially wrecked three houses and totally wrecked four more. In addition, three shops and a pub were also damaged. There were no damages to Government building or munitions works, which were presumably its targets. One local wrote to friends about that night. (2)

> '80 Lamcote Grove, Trent Bridge
> 25 October 1916
> Dear Annie and Frank
> Did you get to know that we had the Zepps at Nottingham a few weeks ago? I shall never forget the row and the awful feeling it gives one. We might have known they were expected and been prepared because the current was cut off at the works. And Bert came home early also the buzzers had blown. But we forgot and went to sleep. I woke up hearing a terrific explosion. It sounded just outside our window but was in Arkwright Street. Bert jumped out of bed and looked through the window. He said he could see the flashes in the sky every time a bomb dropped. I could not have moved if anyone had promised me five hundred pounds. I could smell burning sulphur. We heard about twelve or thirteen explosions and then all was still. You can imagine how we felt next morning when we knew that nearly every one had been dropped in Arkwright Street within five minutes walk of us. There was more glass broken than anything. Not much damage to say. You ought to have seen the thousands of people working at the damage. Nearly every shop from here to the market place has broken windows. Two houses were demolished in Newthorpe Street (just alongside where Uncle Steve's pub was), they were searching for bodies when we went out.'

Newthorpe Street Bomb Damage. Courtesy of Nottingham City Council and www.picturethepast.org.uk. NTGM011044

Unfortunately the rest of the letter does not seem to have survived.

Mr Tansley was eleven-years-old at the time of the raids. He saw the Zeppelin above the corner of Alfred Street South, Robin Hood Street and Blue Bell Hill. There was a rumour, he said, that the Zeppelin had followed a train in and brought the Zeppelin to Nottingham instead of its supposed destination of the Chilwell munitions factory.

Sightseers arrived the next day to see the damage for themselves. Some even hunted for souvenirs. Number 32 Newton Street suffered a hit, killing a husband and wife, Alf and Rosanna Rogers, aged forty-four and forty-three respectively. Harold Renshaw of 3 Chancery Place, Broad Marsh was also killed. At the inquest, coroner Charles Rothera stated that the three were murdered by person or persons unknown.

The station masters were invited to attend the inquest and Rothera told them that the jury were of the opinion that the city was exposed to the attack of airships entirely due to the action of the railway companies. They should obey the same lighting instructions as the general public.

On 5 February Nottingham's softer side came to the fore. A pigeon had got stuck in telephone wires and could not free itself. Employees from a business opposite obtained a ladder and one man climbed it to free the pigeon. This fact was recorded in a letter to the *Nottingham Evening Post* highlighting British sympathy for all God's creatures.

Another year of hardship had been endured by Nottingham folk separated from loved ones, devastated by loss of family members, worn out by a combination of work and scarcity of food, but still standing, hanging on, until life improved.

CHAPTER 4

1917: Seeing it Through

Germany began the year by announcing a campaign of unrestricted submarine warfare hoping to cut off Britain's supplies and starve us into submission. This was also the year, in large part a consequence of the German U-boat policy, that the United States entered the war declaring against Germany in April. For most of the population life went on as usual, whether at home or in the trenches. It was hard, food was scarce and loved ones were separated. In true British spirit Nottingham, its soldiers and non-military stuck it out with no idea when their hardship and loss would come to an end. The best they could do was see it through, day by day.

The year would bring new challenges for women, tighter regulations with more prosecutions and more of the usual accidents and family crises. Food regulations appeared and the limited supply of food became a big issue for everyone, specially so for the poor.

Women

The year began well for the women employed by the City Council, as they were given a bonus. This was followed by an increase for female lace workers, mostly those working in their own homes, of one penny per hour. There were also rises for teachers in this year. Even so, women were generally still paid less than men, even for doing the same job as them.

Stubborn bull! Courtesy of Nottingham City Council and www.picturethepast.org.uk. NTGM011052

Other workers were not so happy and went as far as taking strike action. Female cigar workers were reported as having been on strike for two weeks in June, during which time the Battle of Messines Ridge was fought and won by the British and Dominion troops. The use of nineteen large mines preceded the attack and helped, along with the fact that its objectives were limited, to keep casualties relatively low. The cigar workers voted to continue their strikes until their demands were met. They actually wanted a twenty to thirty-three per cent rise on their pre-war wages to bring them in line with similar workers in London and Bristol. The strike affected 350 local cigar workers.

More women were trained to work on the land under the women's land army scheme that began in March. They were given breeches and overalls and a four week training course.

Of course women maintained their traditional roles as nurses too. Lillian Hutchinson was appointed as a charge nurse at the Cedars. This must have seemed incredibly quiet after her days riding up and down behind the lines, in the early months of the war, with a box of bandages attached to her waist. She received many bruises from the box banging on her hip due to the movement of her horse. Lillian had also served on the *Anglia*, a hospital ship travelling to and from Salonika. Whilst the trips out were quiet, the trips back to Britain with the ship full of wounded and dying soldiers, were demanding and exhausting.

Half way through the year Nottingham women were treated to a Mother Craft Exhibition. It was held at the Albert Hall and opened by the Duchess of Portland. The intention was to bring home to the 'uninstructed' person the seemingly unlimited number of opportunities to get it wrong when raising a child. Apparently one of the methods of approved child rearing was to teach children not to mix with the 'evil and debased' so that when those children, in due course, fell in love and married you might expect grandchildren who would be a credit to you.

Bringing in the Harvest. Courtesy of Nottingham City Council and www.picturethepast.org.uk. NTGM011054

Women Window Cleaners. Courtesy of Nottingham City Council and www.picturethepast.org.uk. NTGM010581

Twenty-three year old Rose Waplington was one of many women who seemed to have missed this exhibition. At the end of July, as the Third Battle of Ypres was about to begin, she was given three months for child neglect. She had three children and they shared a house with Rosie's grandmother in Stretton Street. All three youngsters had vermin bites and were undernourished despite the fact that there was sufficient food. Neighbours said they often saw Rose go out and leave the children alone for hours.

Fundraising

Efforts to raise funds for a wide range of charities continued in 1917 and new regulations relating to flag days were introduced to ensure greater uniformity.

At the Mechanics Hall in January child dancers put on a show for the Star and Garter Soldiers Benefit. Among those who attended were the Duchess of Portland and her daughter in law the Marchioness of Titchfield, Lady Victoria Bentinck and the Belgian Countess de Baillet Latour.

The people of West Bridgford saw the results of the previous year's fundraising when the Trent Bridge Pavilion Hospital was gifted a new medical-electrical ward. It was opened by the Duke of Portland, and although the residents and the Freemasons had given generously more funds were needed to finish the ward.

A push for Nottingham to invest in war loans began in February. Farmers were being asked to invest their money as well as being asked to provide much more food. Sir Charles Seeley, the MP for Mansfield, said that the war had developed into a battle of strength and that if people supported the government there would be no doubt as to the result.

Auctioning the Golden Goose. Courtesy of Nottingham City Council and www.picturethepast.org.uk. NTGM010945

On 9 February the Duke of Portland presided at a War Loan meeting and urged those present to back the country. He said that the war was being carried on with increased vigour and war loans were needed to bring it to a 'victorious conclusion'. He talked about being forced to 'unsheathe the sword', which could not be returned to its scabbard until we could be certain that it would not be necessary to use it again for a very long time. He finished by saying that people would have a more certain return for their money with War Bonds than if they had backed one of his horses.

Sheriff's Cricket Eleven. Courtesy of Nottingham City Council and www.picturethepast.org.uk. NTGM011037

Patriotic Fair. Courtesy of L Cripwell and www.picturethepast.org.uk. NTGM002860

Whitsuntide brought the Patriotic Fair. Trades and villages had stalls to sell their wares but it was not certain, just prior to the Fair if beverages would be allowed as the Food Controller had warned that serving anything alcoholic would lead to excess consumption.

Entertainment in the streets around the square was planned, including bands and dancing by children. It was hoped to drape all the stalls in red, white and blue. It was announced that by the Fair made more than £4,000 by 30 May and that not all the money had yet been collected. Traces of the Fair were still to be seen in the Market Square the following day. A marquee had not yet been removed from beside Queen Victoria's statue; inside it was displayed the remains of a Zeppelin.

The YMCA Hut Appeal was launched in October as the third phase of the Ypres offensive began. An inch of rain within forty-eight hours coupled with bombardments had smashed the drainage system and turned the battlefield in to a quagmire. Because of the increase in the size of the army, 130 more huts were needed. Hut week began on 23 October, with Nottingham's target being £15,000. During that week £13,000 was raised from a city of only 250,000 people. Everyone gave from shops and factories to homes and churches. At a time when food was short, families were torn apart and life was much more difficult than it is today, an outstanding amount of money was raised.

Perhaps the highlight at the end of the year was the announcement that the aeroplane that Nottingham's citizens had paid for was in operation at the Front. A record of its operations was being kept but not being divulged, at least for the present time.

Crime

A busy year for the people of Nottingham also meant a busy year for Nottingham's criminals. Serious offences were almost non-existent and white gloves (a sign of no serious criminals to prosecute) were awarded at the Quarter Sessions of the Assizes.

As usual the women of Nottingham provided their fair share of the criminal caseload. On 1 January Joseph Derry was jailed for three years for theft and his sister in law Elizabeth Clay was bound over for receiving the goods that Derry stole as he burgled homes in Gedling and Carlton. He claimed he had served in the South African War and also in the current war where he had been gassed. He stated that he was 'in drink' at the time of the offence. It did not seem to lessen his sentence any! Only the next day Florence Harvey was jailed for deception. She bought a fur coat using a cheque that was not hers and was jailed for six months.

A large proportion of the cases in front of magistrates were for theft. Some arose from pure greed, like the case of Ethel Cooke, who was brought before magistrates for stealing from her friend and co-employee Kate Cragg. They shared a room at the George Hotel. Other cases came out of desperation. A postman from Carlton was given six weeks hard labour for stealing letters. He stated that he could not feed his wife and family on 26s a week.

Some people were constant visitors to the Guildhall Magistrates courts. Gertrude Howard, alias Clements, aged thirty, had been before magistrates twenty-seven times. This time the offence was being drunk in charge of a five-year-old. She was put on probation for two years on condition she gave up the drink.

Even soldiers were not exempt from the magistrates. In February Charles Rimmer was put on probation after stealing £11 from fellow soldier Charles William Wyatt, coinciding with a period when his military colleagues saw the Germans began to fall back twenty-five miles to the strong defences of the Hindenburg line.

All throughout their troubles the residents of Nottingham kept their mischievous sense of humour. Thomas Handley was convicted, along with James Front, of stealing a cycle from the porch of Bromley House Library. Handley was sent to prison. He cheekily offered to be sent to the army instead. The magistrate drily observed that 'they don't want men like you'. Prison it was.

Some of our Nottingham ancestors managed to commit crime without realising they had done so! John and Florence Tidy were charged with trying to obtain monies by deception. Their son, a soldier, had committed suicide and they claimed the value of his effects, the sum of £3.18s.2d. Shortly after that his widow also put in a claim. The parents were not convicted as the magistrates believed that they had not known that their son had married.

Many cases of defrauding the army were brought before the court as mothers and wives overstated the amount their sons and husbands earned in order to obtain a higher separation allowance payment. Harriet Riley of Beeston was fined £2 for this offence.

There were many other charges that attracted fines and prison sentences. Robert Fletcher of Meadow Lane, a butcher, was sent to prison for three months for selling tuberculosis-infected meats; Thomas Shepherd, a coal dealer of Radcliffe Road, West Bridgford, was fined 40s for cruelty to a horse. He then complained that he had to buy a new collar as the police had taken the previous one as evidence.

Robert Turner, of Field Place, Mansfield Road, was jailed for two months for stealing nine stones of soap from his employer, Lamberts of Talbot Street, whilst Thomas Blower, fifty-eight, from Alderney Street, pleaded guilty to being drunk in charge of a pony and trap. This was his sixtieth conviction. He was fined forty shillings or offered one month in gaol.

A Nottingham footballer was sent to gaol for six weeks in Ripon. He stole 5lb of bacon, 7lb of mutton, 3lb of tea, 6lb of sugar and 1½ pounds of butter as well as a Gordon Highlander's kilt!

Child neglect and domestic abuse seemed never to fail to take their turn in the court. Thomas Radford, a collier, was committed for trail at the Assizes after being accused of throwing corrosive liquid over Annie Waldron, his common law wife. She had left him due to his conduct. Over a month later Annie was still an inmate at Bagthorpe hospital. She was led into the dock and was very feeble. Radford told the court that he had accidentally knocked the vitriol out of her hand. The case was adjourned for a further hearing.

Mary McGuirk spent Christmas in prison after being convicted of child neglect. She had three children and worked in a munitions factory earning nineteen shillings a week. Her son earned eighteen shillings a week and she had a separation allowance from the army. Money was not a problem but the house was filthy and cold and the children were hungry. Her husband had arrived home on the day that the police turned up and he was told to make arrangements for the children before his leave ended.

Appeals tribunal

The Nottingham tribunal continued its work of trying to send everyone it possibly could get its hands on to the army.

A West Bridgford man held a certificate exempting him from the army. Bernard Gayton stated that an honest mistake led him to believe that this meant he was exempt from war work. Despite his exemption from the army he was handed straight to it at the end of his court hearing.

John Cook Hogg was appearing in *Somewhere a Heart is Breaking* at the Grand Theatre in Nottingham when police caught up with him. He had failed to turn up at the right time to enlist and the police had trouble finding him as he used a stage name. He was fined £5 and handed to the military.

Just a month later the Tribunal adjourned indefinitely by way of protest at the attitude of the military present in court. A formal complaint was made by the Tribunal to the Government Board. The Tribunal resumed a few days later.

Another actor, Mr. Gifford, was fined forty shillings and handed to the military in May. He claimed not to have received his call up papers. Charles Warner claimed the same reason as his excuse for not reporting when he should have. He was also fined under the Military Service Act.

A great example of how bureaucracy tied itself up in Nottingham came in June. Mr AE Howitt appeared before the court charged with not displaying a form containing the names of all of those eligible for war service who worked for him. Upon receiving a summons he enquired about it of friends who were magistrates. They knew nothing of this form. Howitt then went to the Post Office to get a form but found that they did not have any. Thankfully common sense prevailed and the case was dismissed.

Letter bag

Nottingham's residents have never been slow to voice their opinions. *Nottingham Evening Post*'s letter bag has always been full of comments. It still is. At that time letters were often signed with humorous names, as for instance, a letter on 9 May that criticised the tramway authorities.

'The Tramways Committee wish to economise but of course they won't start with themselves as that would be like admitting they had done something wrong. How much does it cost to run a useless ticket checking system and run practically empty cars behind each other? Signed: Nuf Sed.'

Scarcity of sugar.

'I noticed recently several correspondents complaining that before they can obtain a pound of sugar they are compelled to make other purchases amounting to £1 or £1.10s and yet in spite of this obvious shortage the bakers and confectioners were displaying for sale fancy and expensive sugar coated Christmas cakes. Do you not think it is time that those in authority ought to place some restriction on these luxuries? I am, sir, Euxine (from the Black Sea)

Long Row promenade.

'We think it quite time that attention was brought to the promenading

Albert Ball Memorial Procession. Courtesy of Mrs M Baguley and www.picturethepast.org.uk. NTGM012291

on Long Row. It is a scandal in these times and measures should be taken to prevent it. Nowadays every able bodied person ought to be helping in some way to hasten victory. It makes one's blood boil when one thinks of the hundreds of people idly parading Long Row whilst lives are being laid down to keep them in safety and comfort.
We are, Sir, Canny Scot and Paddy.'

Soldiers and volunteers

Many men left the city during this year of seeing it through to the end and many others arrived in a city new to them for treatment. Captain Albert Ball, the son of Alderman and Mrs Ball, was reported missing in May. He was a fighter pilot with at least forty-four victories to his credit. He was posthumously awarded the VC having already won the Military Cross and Distinguished Service Order with two bars.

America entered the war but was able only gradually to end troops to the Front whilst the battles in Europe continued. Men aged forty-one to fifty were called up and early schemes were put in place for disabled soldiers to learn new crafts.

The Albert Hall Institute, recently converted to a temporary hospital, received its first contingent of patients on 3 January. Most were suffering from Trench Foot.

British and German authorities reached a tentative agreement on repatriating some prisoners over the age of forty-five, although the process never came to much. Unfortunately by the end of February 1917 the exchange of prisoners had drawn to a halt. The Germans were said by the press to have lapsed back into barbarity.

Army volunteer recruiting was still taking place and a special office was opened for the Army Labour Corps, but not everyone was keen to join. For example, Nottingham painter Henry Jackson, of Norwood Road, drowned himself in the canal at Wollaton on the day he was due to report for duty.

General Hospital Park Row. Courtesy of Nottingham City Council and www.picturethepast.org.uk. NTGM011049

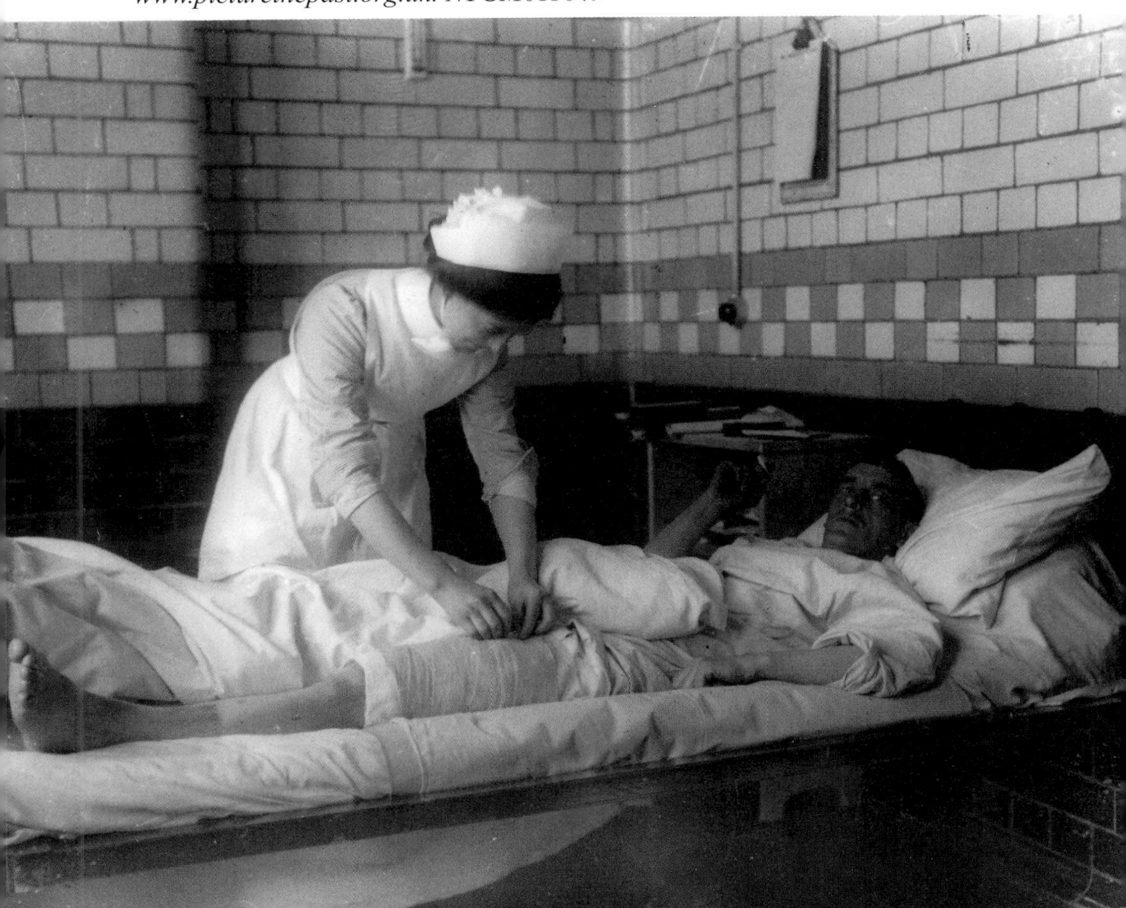

Some who had joined up still found themselves in trouble. Arthur Harrison was wearing a soldier's uniform when he was arrested in the Market Square. He was having considerable success at begging. He changed all the coppers he had been given in a nearby pub and donated ten shillings to the wounded soldier's fund. He had been wounded in France and had had no allowance for eight weeks. He told the magistrates he would be better off wielding a gun in France than a needle in Bagthorpe gaol. He was sent to prison.

The Duke of Portland rewarded Nottingham's volunteer regiments with a gift of drums. They were presented in July at a parade on the Forest, emphasising the importance of a band in fostering army spirit.

Nottingham was chosen in June to be the East Midlands centre for the late Lord Roberts scheme to retrain disabled soldiers. The workshops would provide places for 300 - 400 men, which does not seem many places given the number of wounded arriving in Nottingham's hospitals.

Inspection of volunteers by Duke of Portland. Courtesy of Nottingham City Council and www.picturethepast.org.uk. NTGM008778

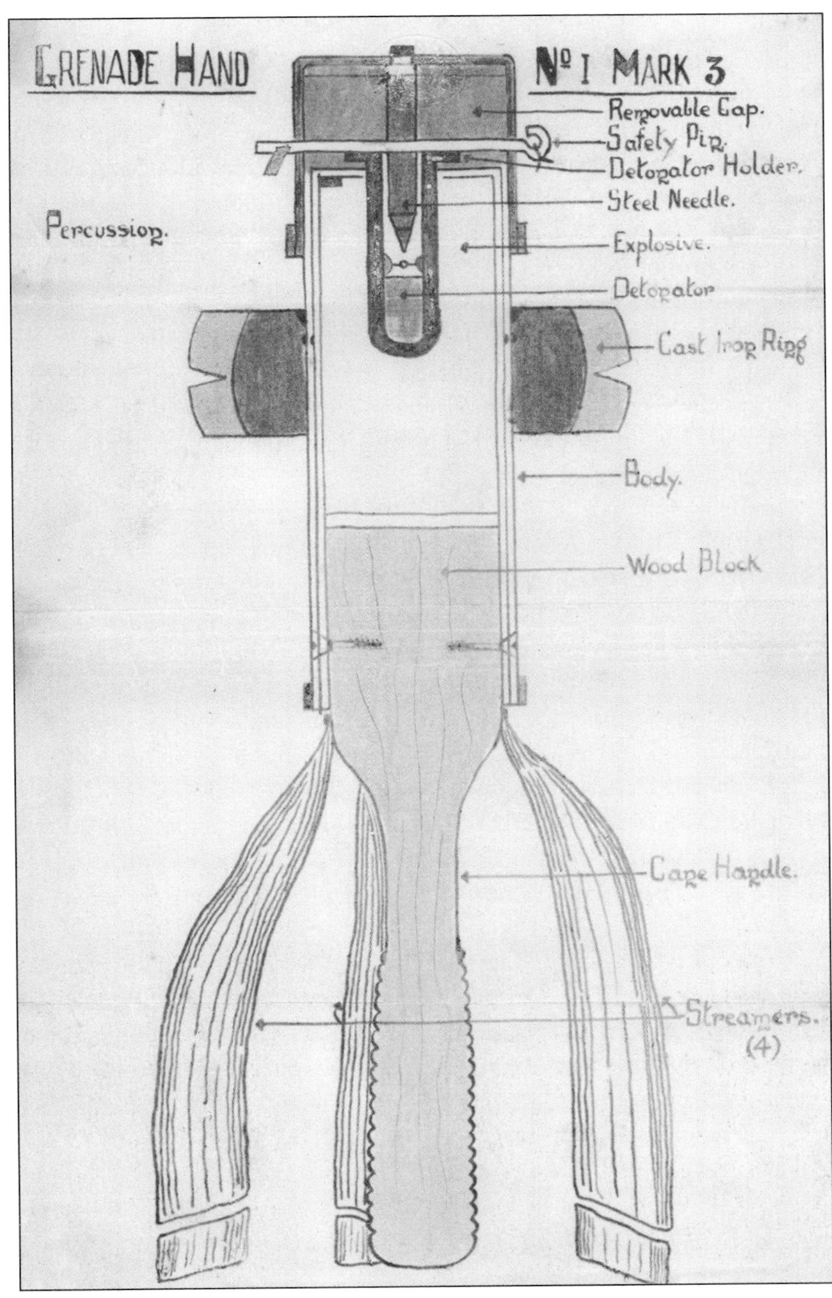

Grenade Diagram by R Pegg. Courtesy of Nottinghamshire Archives. DD 1280 4-3

Food

Food became a major concern in 1917. Numerous new regulations were introduced and not surprisingly many people fell foul of them. Prices rose and the amount available of all types of food was reduced. A rush for sugar was described as selfish and unpatriotic. In addition to a short supply of various food stuffs, great quantities of what was produced was purchased by the military for feeding the troops. The Food Controller for each area found himself wielding substantial power as a result of the new regulations.

Gardens were dug up to be used as allotments and ways were considered to achieve an equitable distribution of essential items amongst the local population. Home owners were also encouraged to keep pigs, whether they lived in a town or in the country and to feed them on kitchen waste.

Many grocers initiated their own rationing before it became compulsory. In March some grocers allowed their customers only 1lb of potatoes each. As a result demand for parsnips and turnips increased, allowing some grocers to charge exorbitant prices for them.

Household sugar was carefully shared out by the shop owners and the public were warned that if they were suspected of hoarding sugar the police would apply for a warrant to search their home. Shop keepers continually refused to serve anyone who was not a regular customer.

Of course, there would always be those who tried to skirt the rules or make extra profits wherever possible. One such man, Henry Price of Mayfield Grove, was fined £3 for overcharging for his potatoes. The court said he had made too much profit for the times they were living in.

Potatoes were again the topic of conversation at a Council meeting held on 11 April; fifty tonnes had been taken by the military and sent to Scotland. Alderman Heath, when addressing the meeting, said that he thought that this was incredible when local people had to queue for theirs with no guarantee of receiving any and especially when our own military hospitals were short.

The end of April saw a campaign for food economy in Nottingham. In the basement of the Prudential Building on King Street a display was given of food stuffs and substitutes and how to cook economically.

Prices of almost everything rose this year as well. The price of tea rose, along with the price of mutton and in May tobacco went up two pence an ounce.

The Local Government Board gave powers to Local Authorities to enforce food regulations. It was decided that sanitary inspectors could enforce these new regulations.

Orders were made, such as the Brewers Sugar Order; the Potato Crop Order; the Feeding of Game Order; the Swedes Order; The Tea Order; the Public Meals Order; and the Cake and Pastry Order.

Also in May the price of cheese increased and fixed meat prices were being considered. There was even a shortage of beer in Nottingham, with the provision of stout and ale becoming critical. On 30 May many pub landlords had to close their doors early, having run out of supplies over the bank holiday. They would not be allowed to replenish their stocks until the following Saturday.

In August it was announced that sugar cards would be introduced in Nottingham to ensure fair distribution. Along with every other piece of legislation, this meant an increase in the bureaucracy needed. Food committees were set up to register grocers and other shops and administer the distribution of sugar cards to households. After 1 October, anyone not registered would not be allowed sugar. Although the scheme was being prepared it was not to become effective until the New Year. Penalties for fraud would be fines and hard labour. On August 16 the *Post* reported that setting up the food distribution committee would cost £2,500. Deputy Town Clerk JH Richards was appointed Executive Officer, with an office in Byards Lane, Bridlesmith Gate.

The weather did not help at all with the worrying food situation. In August fruit and other crops were damaged by heavy rainfall and high winds.

A disease of the potato crop brought allotment holders Harry Chapman and George Cross to the attention of the court in October. AC Cole, of the Intelligence Division of the Board of Agriculture (yes, really!), prosecuted. Outbreaks of disease should have been reported immediately and these two had not. The court decided that there was no evidence that they had wilfully broken the law; neither man had seen a notice about reporting the disease and neither knew where to report it. The court fined them only five shillings each.

As more people took up the call to grow their own food, more land was needed. Fourteen acres along the Victoria Embankment were provided for the purpose. The Minister for Agriculture visited Nottingham as part of this campaign and addressed a meeting in the Albert Hall, saying that victory would go to the side who could command the last ounce of wheat and the last stone of meat. In the last week of December JG Small, Mayor of Nottingham, ordered that no one person should be served with more than half a pound of butter. Although this did not solve the problem, the queues eased and a fairer distribution was achieved. The mayors of practically a century ago seemed to have a lot more power than the mayors of our current times. At a public meeting on New Year's Eve, held to appeal for food economy, Mayor Small told those assembled that the government should follow the example of Nottingham and indeed other cities by setting up a rationing scheme.

It surprised the author to discover that there was no food rationing scheme in place from the beginning of the war although it must have been an enormous learning experience for everyone, it being the first time that the whole country was affected by war.

Family and children

Family life was strained with husbands and sons at war, food in short supply, fuel in short supply and women left at home to cope whilst often also working and doing their bit for the war effort. Cracks in family units were magnified and played out through divorce or violence or sometimes both.

The year did not start well for Mrs Henry Carnill, whose husband was granted a decree of divorce due to her drunkenness. He claimed she was never sober for a week and that she had stabbed him in the eye with a screw driver. Mrs Carnill claimed she was never drunk and that her husband was just excitable.

Another domestic argument arrived before the court in June, when Kathleen Taylor, of Henry Road, West Bridgford, brought her veterinary husband, William, of Clumber Street, Nottingham, to meet the judge. They had been separated for three years and Kathleen claimed that as she and her sister were looking in a shop window in Clumber Street. William came over to her and used obscene language and said that he would like to smash her face in. He refuted this, stating that he crossed the road to avoid her whenever he saw her coming. Evidence was brought that the telephone department had threatened to cut her off if she persisted in ringing up her husband in the middle of the night just to annoy him. Case dismissed.

Florence Keward was granted a separation order from her husband, Garnet Keward, together with twenty-five shillings a week and custody of their two children. He had left his wife as she did not pack him enough food for his lunch and admitted hitting her when she shouted at him to give her more money.

The year did not end well for Edmund and Ellen Crofts, who were sentenced to six months hard labour each. They neglected their four children, aged four to eight, who had five odd boots between them. Money was not the issue, as he earned forty-four shillings a week and had a twelve shillings a week soldier's pension.

Other family traumas also played out in the homes of Nottingham people. A Nottingham hosiery man, John Henry Shaw, of Dunscome Street, St Ann's Well Road, had pains in his hand and increasing blindness. He was afraid of getting caught in the machinery at work and such was his despair that he hanged himself.

John Swift, formerly a butler, also plunged the depths of despair and could not face going back to the war. He had been in hospital for a hernia operation. He had written to his mother pleading with her to come and visit him. The letter had not been posted and was found in his pocket after he committed suicide by drinking carbolic acid.

As if these pressures were not enough, food prices kept rising due to shortages and living expenses continued to increase. A rate rise was introduced in May to cover all the bonuses paid to Corporation employees. At the end of the summer gas prices rose, whilst coal prices were fixed by Nottingham City Council in October. Some relief was felt when it was announced that 2,000 tonnes of coal would be stored for distribution to the poor over the coming winter. Unfortunately it was only to be used if the stocks of coal dealers ran out.

Children's essays in response to a request by the Education Authority provided a unique view of the war. The children said they had to use less soap and wear old clothes; were not allowed to give bones to the dog as they made lovely gravy; and children were not allowed to kick stones, as it would wear their boots out.

A scouts' rally at Trent Bridge cricket ground in July was attended by 1,200 scouts. Colonel Sir Lancelot Rolleston attended with Lady Rolleston and Lady Boot. Lady Bowden gave out the prizes.

One of these scouts, Robert Pegg, aged fourteen, kept a scrapbook cum diary with cigarette cards of generals and admirals.[(1)] Sir Douglas Haig and Sir John Jellicoe featured amongst his collection. Pegg made many sketches of trenches, grenades and tanks. His notes were interspersed with the odd fraction sums and a few cartoon drawings. He also made his own reports of battles, kept newspaper cuttings and foreign stamps. It presents a truly fabulous snapshot of the time.

Prosecutions

The wheels of local bureaucracy kept on turning to keep everyone at home under control whilst the government similarly kept control over those serving abroad.

Under the Defence of the Realm Act Regulations, shops had to close by 8pm. GW Brewitt, a tripe seller (whose occupation has now disappeared), was brought to court as a test case. He was accused of selling ham and dripping after the permitted time. Brewitt claimed he was justified in selling the food as it was newly cooked and, therefore, an exemption to the rule. His business served a poor district with many ladies calling in on the way home from their munitions work. The bench stated that the order was not meant to prove a hardship to national workers. Judgment was given for the defendant.

Messrs Arthur and Henry Homes, wholesalers of Hucknall Road, were not so lucky. They were fined £3 for selling dripping that had been watered down. They claimed that the water had come from gravy added to the dripping at the request of their customers. Many milk sellers also found themselves on the wrong side of the courts.

John Knighton was fined £5 for selling milk that was forty per cent water and Frank Simpkins of Gedling Street was fined ten shillings for exposing milk for sale in a way that it could become contaminated. He had the milk in an uncovered bowl next to a bowl with decomposing onion and beans. Yuk!

When Arthur Dexter of Cinderhill was brought before the court for selling adulterated milk, he said it was raining heavily on the day his milk was tested and that every time he took the lid off to serve some milk more water got in! He was given a nominal ten shillings fine.

Several grocers were fined, in June, for selling seed potatoes to unauthorised persons. They included Frank Dobney, Charles Kirk and Gertrude Hamblin, all of whom were fined forty shillings.

Dairyman Arthur Dexter was again before the court in October for his sixth appearance. This time he was fined £10 to deter him from re-committing this offence. It did not work and he would soon be before the court again.

PC Stebbing, whose wife is also mentioned in this book, stopped Frank Lee, of Radcliffe Road, West Bridgford, on Arkwright Street. He was driving a motorcycle at a speed which endangered pedestrians and other vehicles. Lee was fined forty shillings. The speed? Twenty-five miles per hour.

A new piece of legislation came into force on 1 November restricting fuel for motor vehicles. Since April no licences for the purchase of fuel had been granted to purely private and pleasure vehicle owners. This would now be extended to motor vehicles used for hunting, shooting and golfing. Prosecutions would follow, although motorists would get around the regulations by using commercial licences or buying fuel that had been altered in some way.

Business

Local business kept as busy as ever during the war and some had already begun to think about peace time.

In July the Nottingham Association of House Builders was formed. It opposed all government schemes and called for more and better housing in the city. The Association believed that the only way to achieve this was through their federation.

The Trades Union Congress meeting that year argued that if the workers had better conditions and facilities production would be increased. After the war working hours should be reduced to forty-eight hours per week without a reduction in pay.

Meanwhile an enormous pay increase demanded by Nottingham Corporation employees met strong opposition. Increases of one shilling and six pence were requested for shift workers. This would mean finding an extra £52,791 per year. If all workers, not just union members, were granted this rise a further £20,000 would have to be raised.

Home workers' wages in the lace trade were also under scrutiny. Although they had recently received an increase it had not yet brought them up to the minimum wage. Given the high cost of food, they still did not have enough to live on.

In September Nottingham and Derby tram workers went on strike. They had applied for an increase in wages and accepted the Corporations' offer. The walk-out came as one man was dismissed for insubordination and his colleagues showed their support.

Even the publicans had had enough and threatened to strike. The brewers wanted to charge them ninety shillings per gallon whereas the publicans claimed Burton brewers would sell the same for eighty shillings. The brewers claimed that only a few barrels sold in Burton were eighty shillings, most were ninety shillings. In addition, their Nottingham landlords had a discount of eighteen shillings making it almost the same as the lowest Burton price. Part of the problem for landlords was that they could only obtain two thirds of what they sold in 1916 due to new laws. A meeting was held and a strike averted through a temporary price agreement.

One local business that was doing well out of the war was Digby Colliery. The demand for coal was enormous and their profits rose to £123,863.6d.0d from the sum of £67,665.14s.5d the year before, almost double.

Miscellaneous

In early January the *Post* reported upon an article in the *Telegraph*. A neutral living in Kiel since the war began told of German factory workers who had complained of bad treatment and lack of food. They were sent to the Front.

A group of 1,350 children were given breakfast on the stage of the Hippodrome, around 700 of them children of the Sherwood Foresters. There were six sittings of jam sandwiches, meat sandwiches, scones, cakes and tea.

27 January was the Kaiser's birthday, which the *Post* marked with a feature called 'The Blond Beast'. They said that his birthday should see 'a procession of all those he has murdered rise up against him'.

Air raids in January led children to relate their own experiences. One child said 'the bombs dropped and a lot of people came into our house in just their night clothes. It was a dreadful sight.' Another boy told how his father was so frightened by the raids that he ran all the way to the 'beer shop and hid under the counter'.

The mood changed to celebration in May with Empire Day. The King's Proclamation called for food economy by reducing consumption of wheat and bread and abandoning the use of flour, unless in bread, by one quarter of the pre-war consumption. The King charged all ministers of religion to read out the Proclamation for four successive weeks.

By the beginning of August holiday time had come around and it was reported that Skegness had not been so full for twenty years. It was also said that 'not a bed was to be found' in Mablethorpe or Sutton on Sea, the traditional holiday destination for people from Nottingham. Others ventured further afield, to Blackpool, Matlock and Scarborough.

The Munitions Tribunal continued its work. Harold Daykin and George Dodd were fined fifteen shillings each for being the worse for liquor whilst on duty at work.

William Todd had left Messrs Sands of Colwick and was employed by Messrs Abbot and Lane, confectioners. Sands claimed he was engaged on war work and could not be released, he drove a cart moving essential items for munitions. Abbots and Lane were fined £8 reduced to £4 if Dodd was released to his previous employer within fourteen days.

In January the Picture House showed *Battle of the Alps*, an official Italian war film. Queen Alexandra had watched the film a few weeks before-hand and local people were urged to do the same.

Conditions were arctic-like in the first few months of the year. In

January Grantham Canal at West Bridgford was iced over solid enough to skate on and snow fell on 10 April.

Bankruptcies of 1917 blamed on the effects of war included a lace manufacturer, a stone merchant, the Empress Picture House and another picture house in Beeston run by Edgar Lyman.

A meeting of the Nottinghamshire County War Committee declared that increased production from land could only be secured by giving farmers a minimum price guarantee.

Sheep shearing was identified as a potential problem and it was hoped that skilled workers home from the war on leave or because of sickness could be used to help out.

The Executive Officer to the War Agriculture Committee started an experiment in Nottinghamshire. A caterpillar tractor on a farm in Retford used an eight furrow plough with another four furrow plough attached. The aim was to speed up ploughing of waste land to be able to grow more crops.

Accidents continued in this year also. The premises of Reddish's in the Lace Market were completely destroyed by fire. All of the stock and the company books were destroyed. The company on the floor below suffered around £5,000 water damage to their own stock.

Tramway accidents also continued. A tram coming down Derby Road was thought to be out of control, as there had been an issue with braking. A man on the upper deck yelled that the tram was out of control. Several women jumped off the tram and were injured. Those who remained on the tram were unhurt as it was brought safely to a stop.

1917 had been another tough year for Nottingham folk, with higher prices, more shortages and bad weather all trying their patience. But like every year previously, the people of Nottingham gritted their teeth, dug their heels in and refused to be broken.

CHAPTER 5

1918: The Final Blows

1918 was the final leg of the war for Britain although this seemed an unlikely outcome at the beginning of the year. Fundraising was still taking place as were food restrictions; crimes were still being committed; accidents still happened; and men still lost their lives overseas.

Soldiers and volunteers

Mary Pell, a married woman of King's Meadow Road, was fined £2 or fourteen days in gaol for hiding a deserter. The Australian man was found under her bed wearing her husband's clothes whilst he was away serving at the front.

A total of approximately 1,000 wounded men arrived in Nottingham in the last week of March. They were dispersed from Victoria Station to several local hospitals. As fast as the wounded arrived in Nottingham more men were called up and left. Some young miners did not wait until their groups were called, they were already fit enough to go straight away, and their eagerness was taxing recruiting staff to the limit.

Our local police force was being depleted by men being called up; and men of forty-three to forty-five were sent for medicals after the Government raised the upper age limit. Volunteer soldiers were still

American Troops London Road. Courtesy of A P Knighton and www.picturethepast.org.uk. DCHQ504593

being trained in local parks in April as the 1918 Battle of the Somme, which had caused such a scare as the Germans made big advances, came to an end.

Many wounded soldiers who came from Nottingham ended up in Bagthorpe Hospital, now known as the City Hospital. Mr A Bramley from Queen Street Hucknall had an autograph book in which he encouraged patients and staff alike to make entries. Some entries were poignant, others amusing. Private Harry Corrigan of the Light Infantry wrote, 'What shall I write, what shall it be? Only two words, remember me.'

Private H Newton wrote from Ward 14.

'Forget not him that dies
When peace shall reign once more
Remember still that lonely grave
Beyond some foreign shore
Not marked by marble cross
Maybe not marked at all

Just buried 'neath a grass grown sod
In the place they saw him fall
That death that came too soon
With manhood just but won
He lost his all in his fall
A mother lost a son.'

The British sense of humour always found a way to express itself. Private W Smith of the Coldstream Guards was more down to earth than Private H Newton. He wrote, 'It's a long lane that has no pub in it.'

Corporal Woodman RAF, on Ward 14, also showed his sense of humour:

'There was a young lady from Jhoppa
Who came a society cropper
She went to Ostend
With a gentlemen friend
And they tell me the baby's a whopper!'

Patients at General Hospital. Courtesy of A P Knighton and www.picturethepast.org.uk. DCHQ500518

German Gun in the Market Square. Courtesy of A P Knighton and www.picturethepast.org.uk. DCHQ502738

Nottingham tramway committee explained the effect that the war had had on their staff. 322 had joined up, of whom sixteen had made the ultimate sacrifice. A further 220 men had left the trams for munitions work and had been replaced by 190 women.

974 soldiers worked on the land in June of that year. The labour officer FH Heald stated that if soldiers knew of any men being called up who had experience of the kind they should give him their names and he would try to ensure that they were enlisted in the Labour Corps, who provided soldiers for the land.

A meeting of Nottingham City Council urged that local governments should provide schools where injured and disabled soldiers could learn trades and crafts so that they could earn a living after the war. Alderman Huntsman said that the government should pay for this as they were the ones who compelled the men to fight.

Accidents

A large proportion of the accidents occurring during the year were fire related. Beginning in January Fitchett and Wollacot's premises on Popham Street caught fire. Three engines turned out but had to pour hot water onto their ladders to get rid of the ice before they could use them.

A hosiery factory was completely gutted in February, the third fire in five days. The stock of hosiery and the oil spattered floor helped to fan the flames. Thomas Walker of Gamble Street spotted the flames as he left for work. Neighbours rushed to help carry out furniture and valuables from the three houses nearest to the factory and to offer shelter to those householders. The *Post* estimated the damage to be around £40,000.

The Lambert Bleaching Works on Talbot Street suffered losses in the thousands as well as Snaith and Company's paper warehouse on London Road; both were completely destroyed in separate blazes.
Fire was not the only thing to bring tragedy to Nottingham. CF Daft and his son CF Daft junior, both well known local sportsmen, were lost on the *Leinster* when it was sunk by a German submarine. Both were travelling salesmen for Thomas Adams, Nottingham lace manufacturers. Attendees at the funeral included members of the Masons, representatives of several lace factories as well as members of the local athletics club and representatives of the High School attended by CF Daft Junior.

Crime

Aside from the accidents that caused chaos and upset, criminals also did their best to knock the city's equilibrium off balance.

On 4 January Annie Wolsencroft was given three months in gaol for stealing. She had taken up seven positions in different households and stolen from every one of them. The following day Lily Curwood was given two months for being drunk and idle. Her income was £2 per week and her rent only three shillings but her children were badly clothed and undernourished.

Private detective John Cole was accused of fraud in February. He took money from the public on the pretext of investing it in his company. There was no company and, despite his pleas of innocence, he was sentenced to fourteen months hard labour. It transpired that he had been gaoled in Liverpool for a similar offence and had seventeen other complaints of a similar nature against him.

Other crimes of greed were also common during this year. In March when fighting on the battlefields promised to be critical, William Fewkes' jewellery shop on Parliament Street was broken into. Between £200 and £300 worth of stock was taken. Later the same month cigars and cigarettes were taken from a Nottingham factory. Charles Dixon, a soldier, was charged with theft.

A newspaper vendor who was found begging was fined ten shillings. It seems an insignificant fine given that he had £40 in his pocket and prompts the question why was he begging? Mary Smith of Waterloo Promenade had to endure three months imprisonment despite being the only breadwinner in her family. Her husband had left her when he declared himself bankrupt. She had her widowed mother, her out of work sister and her two children to provide for. She stole postal orders and treasury notes amounting to more than £32. What she initially took to help out the family then became easier and her greed took over, the theft only stopping when she was caught.

Greed was also the downfall of Cyril Drury of Colwick Vale. He was a probationer at the office of the railway. He was given a different sort of probation after he was convicted of stealing 2,300 cigarettes, 12 ½ lb of tobacco and 12 lb of tea belonging to the Great Northern Railway and 18 lb of tea, 26 lb of butter, 17 lb of tobacco and 2,000 cigarettes belonging to the Great Central Railway. Mr Clayton, the defending solicitor, said the railway systems were defective and partly to blame, given that he got away with so much for so long. He was put on probation for three years on condition he joined the navy.

Other crimes were driven by love coming hand in hand with jealousy. Eleven-month-old Evelyn Foster Pole was found dead in a dolly tub in Carlton. Thomas Pole was charged with her murder. Evelyn was the daughter of Thomas' wife Frances, conceived and born whilst Thomas was in the trenches. When he came home the baby was there and his wife had sold the contents of their house. He'd drunk two pints of beer and a bottle of stout the day he killed Evelyn. He said he wished he'd drowned his wife as well. At his trial he wore his uniform and his

Distinguished Conduct Medal. CA Curdy prosecuting said that he found it painful to prosecute a man in uniform. Although the judge said he would welcome any recommendation for mercy the jury found Pole guilty, leaving the judge with only one option: to put on the black cap of death. After a petition raised 18,000 signatures his sentence was commuted.

A different kind of jealousy led to the death of an eight-year-old girl, whose body was found by chance in the outhouse of an abandoned dwelling on Vickers Street, fifty yards from her home on Sycamore Street. A woman on her way home went to use the outhouse facilities and found the girl. Rosalind Adkin had been missing from home for a few days. Rosalind's brother Frederick was charged with her murder. After a medical examination it was said that twelve-year-old Frederick was not responsible for his actions.

Perhaps the most shocking case of the year was that of the Reverend John Godsell Prentice (a great name for a man of his profession) and his wife Hilda. He was a vicar at Tollerton but also worked at a munitions factory. Mrs Prentice worked in the factory canteen one day a week. Between them they devised and implemented a scheme to steal meal tickets and re-use them so Reverend Prentice did not have to pay for meals. Between 500 and 600 tickets were found at their home. Mrs Prentice did not appear in court with her husband. Her doctor said she was 'more or less in a swooning condition'. After six weeks in prison Mr Prentice was released and immediately appeared in court to support his wife. She still looked ill and managed to faint fairly quickly. Mr Prentice's bankruptcy was also heard in court that day. In March, the same month that Soviet Russia concluded a separate peace at Brest Litovsk with Germany and her allies, Prentice was deprived of his benefice at Tollerton by the Bishop of Southwell.

It was another busy year for the courts in Nottingham.

Family life

The continuation of the war and with no end in sight, continued to place a great strain on family life. During a very cold winter the gas company issued flyers urging economy as the government had taken most of the stock of gas.

Reunion at Midland Station. Courtesy of Nottingham City Council and www.picturethepast.org.uk. NTGM011088

In April, as British sailors carried out raids on Ostend and Zeebrugge, the National Service Department urged the public to stop painting, whitewashing and cleaning. They said 'dirty walls and ceilings are in these days evidence of patriotism'. At the end of the same month Nottingham experienced a tuberculosis outbreak. There was no relief at that time and all that many could do was wait for death.

Mosquitoes became the biggest pest in late summer, with hundreds said to be suffering from bites, in some cases to the extent of 'complete prostration'. Dr Boobbyer said the mosquitoes had got worse due to the number of soldiers in the country recuperating from malaria.

The Spanish flu epidemic followed although it was said not to be as bad here as in other parts of the country although by the time October came around many cases proved to be fatal. Dr Boobbyer, medical officer for Nottingham, advised people to go to bed and stay there until they were better. He said contact with others would spread the disease.

Dr Boobbyer Health Officer. Courtesy Nottingham University Hospitals NHS Trust Archives.

He also warned that houses should be well ventilated and places of entertainment closed until the epidemic was over. Some schools had to be shut and the General Hospital had to close to visitors. Forty-six people died at the beginning of November in the same month as German sailors mutinied and Armistice talks began in a railway carriage at Compiegne. By the end of that month Nottingham had the highest death rate from 'flu in the country – just as the carnage of war had ended, this disaster struck the City.

Perhaps the most affecting act of the year came in Nottingham during October. Mayor of Nottingham JG Small presented the DSO to the widow of Major Leslie Collins Woodward, RFA. This honour was usually given by the King but Mrs Woodward had requested that the mayor performed the honour. The mayor pinned the emblem of honour onto the chest of the major's two and a half year old son. The child then saluted the mayor. And there was not a dry eye in the Exchange Building.

Food

Also greatly affecting family life was the continuing poor food situation. Supplies of food were short and government rationing came into effect in 1918. In January, when rioting broke out in Vienna and Budapest, as the inhabitants displayed their dissatisfaction with the war, the *Post* reported that meat was 'almost as scarce as blackberries in February'. Queues were seen outside many shops, with some letting only one customer in at a time and others closing early, as they had nothing to sell. The price of rabbits being sold on the market rose to six pence for two, apparently an unprecedented amount.

The Nottingham Food Control committee sent a plan for the distribution of tea, sugar and margarine to Lord Rhondda, Minister for

Food, for approval. It was agreed and put into place very quickly. To try and help matters further, communal kitchens were initiated with the first one opening in January. The Prudential Buildings on King Street were kitted out for this purpose although there were difficulties in obtaining supplies of crockery and cutlery. On the first day of opening the kitchen took £2; by the following Thursday the amount had risen to £8. Only a month later two more kitchens had been opened with plans for ten more by the end of the following month.

The shortage of food brought a two-sided reaction from the people of Nottingham. Those with little money vented their anger in the Market Square. As some women were refused even a small amount of butter, one woman was then served a pound of it. Local police resolved the situation when they told the stall holder to sell everyone only a small amount. Others queued patiently outside shops, just waiting their turn, starting from as early as 6 am outside some shops. The fact that this was February and it was raining shows the level of desperation.

Those with more money took to hoarding, a complaint brought to the attention of the *Post* by an un-named prominent local merchant. In his store alone one man asked for a whole ham whilst a woman came in asking for tea when she already had some in her shopping basket. The merchant went on to wonder why people would not buy cocoa, soup powders or tinned meats when the stock of those items was plentiful.

Food was also controlled in local cafés and restaurants. On Wednesdays and Fridays from January, under the Public Meals Order, no meat could be served, milk was only allowed as part of a beverage and if you wanted sugar in your tea you had to provide your own.

National Rationing cards came into operation in early February. Items like tea, butter and margarine could not be obtained without a card. Lord Rhondda gave an amnesty to hoarders all over the country by allowing them a week to hand over their excess goods without being prosecuted. In addition they would be given half the net proceeds of the sale of their goods. Police officers were also given powers to apply for a search warrant if they thought a householder was hoarding food. These were drastic measures in desperate times.

Communal Kitchen. Courtesy of Nottingham City Council and www.picturethepast.org.uk. NTGM011084

Rationing brought other problems too. In several places there was a glut of certain foods which were not allowed to be sold, yet fines would be levied for letting food go to waste. Carrots and potatoes were rotting in the ground as there was no-one to harvest them. In April, another unnamed local merchant informed the *Post* that there was a surplus of bacon and it was in danger of going bad as he was not allowed to sell it.

Some food stuffs that were available were not fit for consumption. Dr Boobbyer warned that the milk arriving in Nottingham once a day was not fit for human consumption as it had a sour taste. However, he did endorse eating horsemeat, which was then sold under licence. The shortages of food exacerbated the year's 'flu epidemic as the population's immune systems were weakened by lack of nutrition; there were 194 'flu deaths in November alone.

Fundraising

Despite the hardships being endured due to the weather and a lack of food, fundraising continued unabated. Nottingham rose to the challenge once again, knowing that no matter how much they were suffering at home our troops were having a much harder time of it.

The year's efforts began with Tank Week from 21 to 26 January. Films were shown in local cinemas and a tank was parked in front of the Exchange Building. The tank arrived a few days before Tank Week at Midland Station and paraded through the city before coming to rest in front of the Exchange. At the same time the YWCA had a target of £10,000 to raise for huts in Nottingham for womens auxiliary workers.

Only a short time later Navy Week was held. The aim was to raise £800,000 to buy two light cruisers even though the city had raised two and three quarter million pounds in the recent Tank Week. The Duke

Tank at the Exchange. Courtesy of Nottingham City Council and www.picturethepast.org.uk. NTGM010948

Duke of Portland at Baseball game. Courtesy of A P Knighton and www.picturethepast.org.uk. DCHQ504594

of Portland and Mayor Small urged local businesses to pledge their support. Mayor Small hoped to raise enough money to get the name of the City once more amongst the Navy's Fleet, having lost the previous one to enemy action.

At the end of April the money raised by the previous year's Patriotic Fair, a total of £41,609, was distributed. Among the local recipients were hospital supply depots, the Comfort for Troops Fund and Ellerslie House, a home for wounded soldiers.

As soon as the distribution was decided upon it was back to the fundraising. War Weapons Week began on 15 July as the Germans' final attack of the spring offensive failed at the Battle of Marne, causing further irreplaceable German casualties. War Weapons Week was organised by those who organised Tank Week. Gun Week came along in October, and Nottingham people were again asked to give generously.

A Nottinghamshire treasure sale for war charities was given 687 donations to auction. The proceeds would go to help King George's Fund for Sailors, Nottingham hospital's supply depot and Red Cross clothing. At the sale the Duke of Portland bought a red wallet with a war medallion of the Duke of Wellington. He paid £25 for it and then put it back in the auction where it was sold again for £8.

Prosecutions

The increase in regulations relating to food and fuel inevitably brought more prosecutions and the courts were kept busy.

Harry J Monks, aged fifty-eight, was charged with illegally using petrol. He had been seen travelling in Chilwell on Christmas Day and later playing golf. Petrol was not allowed for pleasure trips. He claimed that there was ambiguity in the motor spirit restriction order. The bench disagreed and fined him £1.

Monks was not alone in his dislike of the order. Cotgrave farmer John William Baker was seen in Keyworth with a gentleman and two ladies. He said he had been to Owthorpe to look at timber. The court noted that Owthorpe was in the opposite direction from Cotgrave to that of Keyworth and fined him thirty shillings.

Prosecutions which related to food included Harry Jackson of 183 Radford Road. He was accused of selling potatoes above the set price and without a wholesale certificate. He held a retail certificate but sold potatoes to a woman who was then selling them on. The court decided, therefore, that his act was as a wholesaler. He made more profit than he was entitled to make and was fined three guineas.

In February a West Bridgford grocer was fined for paying too much for butter. The court wished to fine the seller but Lakeland Dairy Company were based in Ireland. Alfred Mansell said he could not buy the butter for any less, despite this he was fined £2 and two guineas costs. Butchers James Arbitrage and Joseph Watson were fined for selling meat at excessive prices. The price of meat had been fixed. Arbitrage was fined £10 and Watson £5. Frederick Hole of Sneinton Hermitage was charged with selling milk that had forty-three per cent water added. He was fined the maximum of £20.

Arthur Dexter appeared in court for the eighth time in May a month when the British launched a second raid on Ostend, this time successfully blocking the harbour entrance. Dexter was accused of watering down his milk. He was not inclined to follow his solicitor's suggestion and get out of the milk business and he was fined £35. Only a month later Dexter was fined again, this time for refusing to provide a sample. As soon as he had seen the inspector approach he took off.

George Broadbent was fined for not displaying prices in his shop. He blamed his wife as she was in charge of the shop that day. It did not help him any, in avoiding a fine.

Perhaps the most shocking case of stupidity came before the court in October. A man who worked in the munitions factory filling shells was fined £10. He had hit the top of a shell with a hammer, causing a spark, despite the procedures set down for handling shells. He was lucky to get away with his life. Four men had died recently due to the exact same action, he was told by the magistrates.

Women

As usual for this time, women had varying experiences in life, although the year started on a positive note with the grant of suffrage to women over the age of thirty. Six million voters had now been added to the electoral register. In the same month the Women's Labour League met just before the Labour Party Conference. The meeting closed with a demand for a Minister for Peace.

A Women's War Work campaign was held at the Exchange with members of the Women's Auxiliary Army Corps and Women's Land Army attending. The Duchess of Newcastle reported that 989 women were working on the land in the county and in June it was reported that women were learning to shear sheep. It was thought that after the war openings for women would include those of teachers and clerks in Italy and France. It would help alleviate the expected high rates of unemployment of women who would vacate their jobs when the men came home.

For some women the year was much the same. Amy Mundy's diary for the year reads as follows [(1)]

January 1 – A very miserable day all day
January 8 – Thick snow on the ground, intensely cold
February 12 – Four years since last operation [Medical operation? For her or a member of her family?]
Mar 7 – Poorly all day. Went to bed at 5 o clock

April 1 – Snowing at times. Went to see the damaged plane in the fields up the lane. [Whose plane was it? How was it damaged? Perhaps it did not seem important enough for her to record.]
April 4 – Cold all day, no one came
April 13 – Baex killed by the 10.26 train at Burton Joyce aged 81
April 27 – Hot day felt tired all day
June 6 – Ma knocked up. Very poorly. [Presumably ill rather than pregnant!]
July 2 – Child fell out of train died on the way to hospital [A tragic accident, although Amy writes about it almost dismissively.]
September 7 – Ma and I went to Skegness
October 24 – Awful fog
Nov 2 – In bed ill
Nov 11 – Armistice signed. Joy all that day. [Even on that momentous day Amy managed to rein in her emotions!]
1919 January 1 – I saw a pheasant in the garden.

Business

Our local firms also had a challenging year, with increased wages and difficult trading conditions. Right from the beginning of the year pay rises were demanded and granted with Nottingham's carters and tram drivers, who benefitted from a £1 a week rise, leading to an increase in fares in March. Fares of one and a half pence rose to two pence and fares of two and a half pence rose to three pence. Other fares were not being raised although the distance travelled for the money was reduced. This caused much controversy and some fares had to be amended. The length of some journeys was restored to their former position and an amended scale of charges was brought in. However, it did not end there as tramway workers demanded a further rise in June. Twelve and a half per cent was sought which seems a huge amount now. Any advance was to apply equally to men and women, although women were only guaranteed work until the men came home and reclaimed their jobs.

The final issue for the tramway managers to face in 1918 was the 'flu virus. In mid-November thirty-four drivers and seventy conductresses were absent from work, causing disruption to the service.

The rise for the tram workers, was swiftly followed by another for the building trade. Their wages were advanced by one and a half pence an hour, although their demand for all overtime to be paid at double time was denied at arbitration.

Wages were not the only issue causing a rift between workers and employers and sometimes between the workers themselves. Thirty youths employed at Barber Walker and Company's pit at Watnall absented themselves from work, resulting in the loss of the production of 5859 tonnes of coal. One of their colleagues who had served in the war now suffered from miner's nystagmus (a rapid pendular movement of the eye) and they demanded that he be removed. Refusal resulted in the youths caming out for four days. They had also been out in May and June for different grievances. The pit almost ground to a halt as the men could not work without the boys. The union men of the pit were against the boys and tried unsuccessfully to get them to be reasonable. All the boys were fined between £3 and £5.

In August, when the allied counter offensive was launched at Amiens, it was the turn of the Cinderhill and Broxtowe pits, both belonging to the Babbington Coal Company to strike. The protest this time was against workmen making over time. Roughly 2,000 tonnes were lost in the few days they were out. Digby Colliery lost 6,000 tonnes of coal when men went on strike there. The colliery claimed compensation from each of the men for the loss of 400 – 500 tonnes which had been lost on a previous day when the miners refused to go down the pit. The men, in turn, refused to go down the pit until the summons were withdrawn. The colliery offered to reduce the amount claimed if the men returned to work. Their solicitors persuaded them to do so.

Of course, no discussion of workers and strike action would be complete without referring to corporation workers. Their demand for more money came in August. They belonged to the National Union of General Workers and their numbers included the water department, works and ways, the electricity department and school caretakers. Each department was paid at different rates and the aim was to unify the pay scale. An application was also made to the Health Committee on behalf of the Eastcroft Destructor men. The Health Committee refused to refer the matter to arbitration and the men gave one week's notice to strike. Unfortunately, ten of the Eastcroft employees declined to turn up for work before the strike was due to start. Between fifty and seventy other men walked out in sympathy. Mr J Terry, manager, tried to persuade the men to return to work. A special committee met on 30 August with a deputation from the men and it was agreed that proposals would be put before the Council if the men returned to work immediately. The deputation was to put the issue to the men that night. The men were collectors of night soil in the city and any walk out by them immediately put the health of the city at risk.

Nottingham's businesses also had other pressures. Alderman Ball, chairman of the Gas Committee, urged shop keepers to close their doors early to try to save fuel. He declared it their patriotic duty. The lace trade had its coal rationed and to receive any at all each company had to register with the coal controller.

Disaster struck in Nottingham on 1 July at the Cammell Laird armaments factory where there was an explosion. 134 people lost their lives on the day of the explosion. It shocked everyone and Private G McDonnell, a discharged soldier, was moved to write: (3)

'A sudden change – they in a moment fell.
They had not time to bid their friends farewell,
Death quickly came – without a warning given
And bid them haste to meet their god in heaven.'

Lottie Martin began working at the factory in 1916 and described the conditions. (2)

'We had to ascend a ladder to man the crane and our descent was by rope when descent was necessary. Imagine this. I was never very brave but this procedure fairly took the cake. Here I was in a predicament I had never visualised. If I failed to mount the ladder I would be out of work and this I could not face. I had my board to pay so up I went but it was some time before I mastered the rope'.

Jessie Whicher, also of Cammell Laird recalled:

'My hours of work were as follows: 7am to 3pm then 3pm to 10pm or 10pm to 7am then there was an arms shortage and a seven day week night shift was 6pm to 7am and the wages were about £2 8s 6d to £2 15s. For a long night shift the pay was about £3 17s. Sometimes I did a few hours of night shift in the paint shop at the end of the factory. There you pushed three shells at a time, oddly coloured shells hanging by grippers with little wheels on an overhead rail, from one part to the end of the shop and the rail trucks. I still remember the strength it took to get and keep those three shells moving.'

The moaning of local firms seems quite petty in comparison to the tragedy at Chilwell and the horrors being lived in the trenches.

Miscellaneous

In the early hours of a January morning a boy of twelve found a heap of silver coins in the gutter in Gamble Street. Other people had also found coins and taken them to the police station. Sixty were found in all. No one had reported a robbery or a loss. The *Post* speculated that they had been left there by an eccentric or by a mentally feeble person. The coins were eventually distributed to those who found them.

In February a rocket was let off from the roof of the Guildhall. It was an experiment for an all clear signal. A crowd of people gathered to watch but only the police stations in St Ann's and Leenside areas of the city heard it, both fairly close to the Guildhall.

Nottingham's very first recycling efforts were recognised in this year. A conference of Health and Sanitary authorities of the East Midlands was held at the Exchange in April. The mayor said there was ample room for the special collection of waste that could be fed to pigs or recycled, such as textiles, paper, glass bottles and stone jars. The National Salvage Council provided lists of people who would buy such waste.

Constance M Jeans of Nottingham found herself the centre of attention, albeit briefly, in mid July when she broke the record for a 220 yard swim in Coventry. She managed the distance in three minutes seven seconds, a second faster than the previous record.

Alderman Ball caught the attention of the *Post* when he bought the whole of Shaftesbury and sold it again in one day in September. It was thought to be the first time that a whole town had been for sale. Presumably Alderman Ball made a worthwhile profit for his efforts!

In the same month as British and American troops pierced the Hindenburg line. Nottingham's public library celebrated its fiftieth birthday, Sir Arthur Conan Doyle (who lost a son in the 'flu epidemic) gave the address at the University College. Tickets were sold for the event with the proceeds going to war charities.

At the appeal tribunal in May, Robert Burton was asked to explain why he had failed to report for duty. He stated that he had a mother to support and that he did not want to become a military controlled murderer. He was handed over to the Army.

Empire Day was celebrated at every school in Nottingham on 17 May. The Chairman of the Education Committee, Alderman Houston, said the 'tradition of our glorious heritage must be handed down from generation to generation'. He said that much depended upon children being trained to become true and loyal citizens and to hold the Empire together and pass it onto another generation 'unimpaired and intact'. One hundred years on, Alderman Houston's vision is a distant memory.

The Armistice

Every event of the last four years was suddenly overshadowed by the long awaited news that the war was over. The last shot was fired at 11am on 11 November 1918, although the war officially ended with the Treaty of Versailles on 28 June 1919.

The news came to the city at 10.34 am and the *Post* reported that within half an hour the city 'was ablaze with bunting'.

Factory hooters blared, church bells rang and people swarmed the streets, many having been given time off work. Many public houses did not open due to a shortage of beer and the fear of riotous behaviour. Crowds collected in the Market Square to celebrate. We still do that now; where else would we go?

The mayor suggested that every blind should be left up and the city flooded with light. Robert Pegg worked at Boots when the Armistice was signed. He was let out of at work at 12.20 pm and with a couple of other boys made fireworks in Boots laboratory with the aid of thermometer cases. He went first to St Mary's Church and then, finding that full, went to St Peter's Church instead. He recorded that the streets were crowded, bunting was waved and the sounds of laughter and

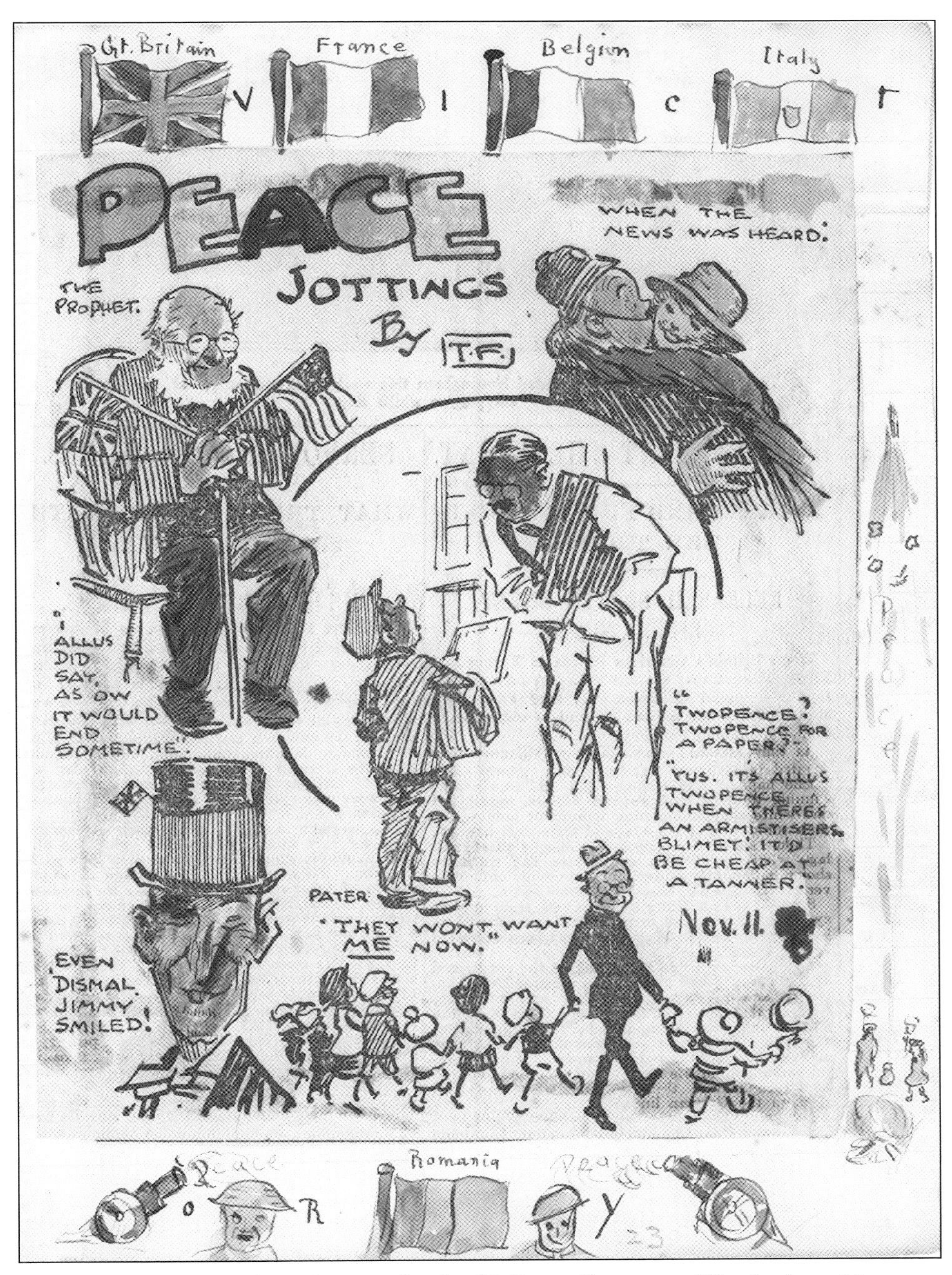

Peace Jottings from the scrapbook of R Pegg. Courtesy of Nottinghamshire Archives. DD 1280-3

Celebrating the Armistice. Courtesy of Nottingham City Council and www.picturethepast.org.uk. NTGM011043

shouting were all that could be heard. He noted that 'the spirit of socialism is prevalent all over the world'.

The last all clear was sounded in the Market Square at just before midnight by the Scouts. A huge sigh of relief was heaved by the city that day.

Of course it would take some time before the men began to return home, before the normal food supply was restored and life in general was returned to normal. But Nottingham had made it through one of the darkest periods in its history and its people had survived. More than that, their spirit was undiminished. Life would never be the same again for Nottingham. And that is just as it should be.

Notes

Chapter One

1. Nottingham and the Great War edited by David Marcombe (Chapter entitled Nottingham People during the First World War by Julie O'Neill) University of Nottingham Department of Adult Education
2. Nottinghamshire Archives Acc No 7978 Box 2L
3. Nottinghamshire Archives DDPL6 18/1
4. See note 3
5. Nottinghamshire Archives DD2455/1-2
6. Nottinghamshire Archives DD748/3
7. Nottinghamshire Archives TA1/1
8. See note 1

Chapter Two

1. Nottinghamshire Archives CATC10/128/9
2. Nottingham and the Great War edited by David Marcombe (Chapter entitled Nottingham People during the First World War by Julie O'Neill) University of Nottingham Department of Adult Education
3. Nottinghamshire Archives DD2455/1-2

Chapter Three

1. Nottinghamshire Archives DD2455/1-2
2. Nottinghamshire Archives M12625/3

Chapter Four

1. Nottinghamshire Archives DD1280 /1-3

Chapter Five

1. Nottinghamshire Archives DD2455/1-2
2. Nottingham and the Great War edited by David Marcombe (Chapter entitled Nottingham People during the First World War by Julie O'Neill) University of Nottingham Department of Adult Education
3. Nottinghamshire Archives DD1749/18 Memorial Card for England's Gallant Munition Girls 1918

Bibliography

Books

First World War and Popular Cinema by Michael Paris, Edinburgh, University Press Limited 1999

Men Women and Things: Memories of the Duke of Portland by the Duke, Faber and Faber 1937

Nottingham and the Great War edited by David Marcombe 1984 (Chapter entitled Nottingham People during the First World War by Julie O'Neill)
University of Nottingham Department of Adult Education

Magazines/Pamphlets

Cammell Laird National Projectile Factory 1915-1917
Cammell Laird National Ordnance Factory 1917-1919
Hucknall Torkard Times Issue 9 December 1998 and Issue 49 December 2008
Nottingham and the Local Press by Peter Foster, *Nottinghamshire Historian* Autumn 2009
Twice Celebrated Peace by Peter Foster, *Nottinghamshire Historian* Autumn 2012
TS Roadley Flying Teacher by David Nunn, *Nottinghamshire Historian* Autumn and Winter 2010

Websites

www.bbc.co.uk/remembrance/timeline/
www.britishnewspaperarchives.co.uk
www.findmypast.co.uk
www.ournottinghamshire.org.uk/

Index